Natural/Unnatural?

JOHN I. CLINE

All rights reserved. No part of this book may be reproduced or transmitted in any form or by any means, electronic or mechanical, including photocopying, recording, or by any information storage and retrieval system without express written permission from the author, except in the case of brief quotations embodied in critical reviews and certain other noncommercial uses permitted by copyright law.

Printed in the United States of America.

Brilliant Books Literary
137 Forest Park Lane Thomasville
North Carolina 27360 USA

Natural/Unnatural?

JOHN I. CLINE

The Monogamy Mystery reflects the personal views and opinions of John I. Cline and is not an initiative of the New Life Baptist Church (*NLBC*) nor does it necessarily reflect the views of the trustees, leadership, management, staff, and members of NLBC.

CONTENTS

Foreword i
Prologue v
Endorsement vii
Introduction The Dialogue ix

Chapter 1: In the Beginning It Was Not So 1
Chapter 2: Is Biology to Blame? 17
Chapter 3: The Sociology of Monogamy 25
Chapter 4: Infidelity in Society 33
Chapter 5: The Mystery of Infidelity 39
Chapter 6: Why Did I Get Married? 47
Chapter 7: Can You Handle the Truth? 67
Chapter 8: Keeping the Wrongdoer; Forgiving the Wrong 71
Chapter 9: God Help Us All: Spirituality 87
Chapter 10: A Word to the Young 99
Chapter 11: Mystery Solved! 111

Epilogue 113
Appendix 117
Afterword 125
About The Author 129

FOREWORD

It is easy to reach a place as individuals where we become satisfied with the status quo. We structure our lives to the point that we can almost predict what will happen from one day to the next. For many, this stability provides a deep sense of security and well-being, and nothing is wrong with that. It is when this type of comfortable living invades our spiritual life that it will cause us trouble.

Life brings us great comfort when we are satisfied with our jobs, homes, financial standing, religion, or beliefs. It's in this life when we become complacent about our personal convictions and satisfied with our spiritual progress that we need to move out of that comfort zone.

We should never reach a place as children of God where we are totally satisfied with our walk and witness to a lost and dying world. I applaud the courage and obedience of my friend and brother, John I. Cline. To know this man of God personally is to respect him as real, relevant, and relational.

Several years ago I met him in Tortola, British Virgin Islands. I sat in conversation with him and knew within ten minutes that he was one who needed to be in my life. I inducted him into my small circle of personal friends who have an eternal impact on my life. Every now and then, one will come into your life not for a reason or a season but for a lifetime. Proverbs 13:20 (NKJV) states, "He who walks with wise men will be wise, but the companion of fools will be destroyed."

Who you choose to do life with determines your future. If you choose to walk with the wise, then according to God's Word you will be wise; but the companion of fools will be destroyed or "will suffer harm" (as translated in the NIV). God has given John I. Cline wisdom beyond his years. According to biblical understanding, he is wise. A wise person is one who sees life for how it is and makes decisions based on how life really is rather than on how he or she hopes it would somehow be.

The Monogamy Mystery is more than thought-provoking. It is a must-read for any belief system, class, religion, or gender. It is sure to make you read and reason at an enjoyable pace. John I. Cline, I believe has been uniquely placed by God as a rare gem and proven trailblazer. This work validates the predestined international platform that is upon his life.

I encourage you to read and receive its contents in its entirety. I love to explore new places of thought, and *The Monogamy Mystery* is sure to take you on an enjoyable journey. The foundation and principles of this book give thought to why so many relationships are suffering. There are many people we associate with who are afraid to release the painful memories of the past and are perhaps forfeiting another chance to live life at its fullest again.

This moment in time is precious. We must vigorously work to avoid regret. Regret is the by-product of refusing to consider wise counsel in order to learn from the examples of others. Regret is the humiliating confession that you've blown it and you know it. Regret is sitting on the sidelines going over and over all of our bad decisions. Getting the chance to wave a magic wand to make it right would be an opportunity none of us would pass up.

What has happened in the past is over and we should grow from it all—be it the good, the bad, or the not-so-presentable. *The Monogamy Mystery* is a magnet for great discussion and fellowship.

John I. Cline, thanks again for stretching many of us yet again and challenging us to leave our comfort zones.

—Bishop Darryl S. Brister

PROLOGUE

First and foremost, let me say that as a born-again believer and senior pastor of the New Life Baptist Church (NLBC) in Tortola, British Virgin Islands, I am not a proponent of divorce. I believe in the sanctity and the institution of marriage! Yet, I have found myself with a biography that factually asserts that I have been married and divorced twice. In the process, I was blessed to have fathered two boys, both from my first marriage.

In my capacity as senior pastor of NLBC, over the last twenty-two years, I have counseled many prior to marriage, during marriage, during the breakdown of the marriage, during divorce, and post-divorce, and I have addressed a plethora of issues plaguing these relationships, marriages, and lives—the most constant of which has been, by far, infidelity.

Infidelity has been a destructive force to the institution of marriage. Many husbands and wives find themselves in the middle of extramarital affairs, not because they want to destroy their marriages, not because they do not love their spouses, and not because they are inherently evil or bad-intentioned.

In many cases, persons admitting to infidelity have no explicable reason to offer for examination. They genuinely regret the behavior and the hurt it causes, yet they may find themselves in the same situation again and again. In counseling many of these people, I have understood them, I have cried with them, I have sympathized with them, and I have empathized with them. I have counseled them on the best ways to prevent infidelity going forward and how to survive infidelity in marriage; yet at the root of the problems that keep rising to the surface, a question consistently resonates: Were we really designed to be monogamous?

I am of the firm belief that knowledge is a door, and information is the key. If persons are adequately armed with the correct information, they can make more informed and intelligent life decisions to their benefit instead of to their detriment. Moreover, having lived the majority of my adult life between the United States of America and the British Virgin Islands, the dual-cultural experience has provided me with a lifetime of sociological experiences, both in an individual and professional capacity and from two different societies and cultures from which I can draw my conclusions.

My total life experiences have brought me to a place where I have formed the view that it has become urgent to unearth some necessary truths and understanding about monogamy and interpersonal relationships in an effort to stop, correct, and guide future generations of persons who opt for committed relationships in their ultimate pursuit of happiness.

I therefore decided to embark on an exciting and truth-seeking journey to encourage a dialogue on this issue of monogamy that has remained a mystery to so many of us for far too long. In communicating the findings of my journey, I was assisted by my writer, Ayana S. Hull, and I express my sincere gratitude and appreciation to her for lending her talent, her time, and her management skills; and for the relentless effort, encouragement, assistance, and dedication she employed in the process of helping me bring this idea to fruition.

ENDORSEMENT

Fasten Your Seat Belts and Enjoy the Read!

When Bishop John I. Cline told me he was going to write a book about monogamy, my first inclination was that it would be presented as a very one-sided, idealistic perspective. I also concluded it would be a relatively short read that reiterated the ideology of the Christian faith supported by laws invoked by the United States of America. However, after reading the book, my dwarfed opinion quickly changed.

In this revolutionary book, Cline gleans from a wealth of knowledge and personal life experiences that unveil a clear panoramic view on the topic. From dissecting issues surrounding the institution of marriage, infidelity, and the ever-popular debate over monogamy as a natural occurrence, *The Monogamy Mystery* provides a thoughtful reflection into the process of belief and human transformation. Readers might want to strap on their seat belts in preparation for digesting Bishop Cline's position on this heavily debated subject.

—Dr. Jamal H. Bryant

INTRODUCTION
THE DIALOGUE

So, what is monogamy?
Monogamy in its strictest sense of definition (which is also its biblical intention) means marriage to one marriage partner or the condition or practice of being married once in a person's lifetime. It is derived from the Greek words, *monos*, meaning "one," and *gamos*, meaning "marriage."

Monogamy as it has been accepted today from a more sociological aspect (social monogamy) can also mean the practice or condition of having a single, sexual partner, either during a person's lifetime (monogamy in its true sense) or during a period of time (monogamy in its serial sense). Similarly, in zoology, monogamy is the practice or condition of having only one mate during the breeding life of a pair of animals (true monogamy) or during the breeding season of a pair of animals (serial monogamy). Against this backdrop, I propose to discuss the mystery of monogamy, and in so doing, my focus will encompass the various accepted definitions of monogamy in the various contexts.

Is monogamy unnatural?
One of the world's biggest unsolved mysteries is the question of whether monogamy is natural. Most of us will find no struggle in accepting that monogamy is certainly uncommon. However, the vexing question with respect to monogamy and where many of us struggle is

whether it is unnatural. Was it really intended and expected for created man (being both man and woman in this context) to be monogamous?

An initial defensive response to this question may be yes, and if you ask that same person to justify his or her response, he or she would probably say that the Bible is authoritative on the point! Yet, in a counter-defense, one may pose a deeper question: Is biblical authority on this issue spiritual authority? What is really meant by *monogamy*, *adultery*, *fornication*, and *illicit sexual relationships* where these terms are discussed in the Bible? Is monogamy a spiritual obligation, or is it a religious and/or regulated social obligation?

Many of us—and the church, in particular—would prefer to dismiss a debate of this nature as it would tend to challenge our theological foundations in many respects. However, dismissing the issue and not tackling this long-standing problem head-on is a mistake and is perhaps one of the reasons marriages in society are in the perpetual chaos that they are in. The purpose of this book is to explore these issues from a natural, physical, biblical, sociological, and spiritual perspective and to offer a panorama of monogamy from my own life experiences.

On the journey, I will:

- explore the various definitions, extrapolations, and permutations of the word *monogamy*;
- address the distinction between the concept of true monogamy and serial monogamy;
- discuss the biblical origin and authority for monogamy;
- illustrate monogamy as it was originally intended and existed in the beginning;
- discuss the initial fall of man and the breakdown of monogamy;
- examine the biology of created man as juxtaposed to the ideals of monogamy;

- analyze and compare the concept of monogamy in society in the ancient/biblical era and monogamy in society in modern times;
- illustrate and illuminate the purpose and importance of monogamy (a) from an individual perspective, (b) in marriage, (c) in the family unit, and (d) in the wider society;
- explain the consequences of monogamy (its advantages and disadvantages);
- underscore the importance of understanding the purpose of marriage;
- present a current synopsis of society's views on infidelity and monogamy;
- provide some guidance as to how created man can stop the fallout caused by anti-monogamous behavior;
- highlight the importance of separating the sinner/wrongdoer from the sin/wrong; and
- offer helpful tips as to how relationships can successfully survive infidelity.

I will then conclude:

- with an in-depth study of spirituality;
- with a critical analysis of the importance of spirituality to the successful practicing of monogamy;
- by providing an answer to the question raised as to whether it was indeed intended for created man to be monogamous; and
- by providing guidance to younger generations to steer their interpersonal relationships in a happy, fulfilling, and successful direction.

The matters discussed in this book will undoubtedly raise questions in the minds of the readers. Couples reading the book together can have healthy discussions from a holistic perspective about one of the biggest problems wreaking havoc on interpersonal relationships. It can bring some level of unfiltered understanding in society among sexual partners (married or unmarried, religious or nonreligious) on sexual behavior.

It will challenge the spiritual beliefs of certain readers and question behavior patterns that some readers regard as normal. However, I must stress that I do not intend for Christian or other religious-type readers to regard the book as a justification to engage in any type of sexual behavior that contradicts the sexual behavior ultimately ordained by God through the institution of marriage.

CHAPTER 1
In the Beginning It Was Not So

Scripture indeed records that in the beginning, God created Adam. After He created Adam, He looked at His creation and said that it was not good for Adam to be alone, so He created a wife for him. Her name was Eve. Many use this creation event, and justifiably so, as biblical authority to support the conclusion that God intended for the union of marriage to exist between one man and one woman. Although this event supports the view that monogamy was the original intention, as later books of the Old Testament are explored, there is an obvious shift from the concept of monogamy during the days of Adam to polygamous relationships in later generations.

As an example, the first instance of polygamy (having more than one spouse) in the Bible was that of Lamech, a descendant of Cain. The Bible records in Genesis that Lamech married two wives – an indication from Scripture that polygamy was perhaps not viewed as immoral, illegal, or condemned by God.

As another example from Genesis, even though Abraham had his legal wife, Sarah, we also see evidence of an extramarital relationship (polygyny), between Abraham and Sarah's handmaid, Hagar. Polygyny is the form of polygamy that occurs between a man and multiple women.

We are aware from scripture there was no legal marriage between Abraham and Hagar and that the extramarital relationship between these two was encouraged by Abraham's wife (who was Hagar's mistress) for a specific purpose only. The benefit was for Sarah to have a family through her handmaid; in today's terms, Hagar would have been a surrogate. Additionally, the relationship between Abraham and Hagar was not intended to be maintained in the sense of Hagar being another wife or partner for Abraham. It was intended to be a purely sexual event for the purposes of reproduction of a child since Sarah, who had concluded that she was barren, had not yet reproduced a child for her husband. As the biblical event illustrates, Abraham did have sexual relations with Hagar; Hagar did become pregnant; and she did give birth to Abraham's firstborn, whose name was Ishmael.

It is important to note that Scripture does not indicate any condemnation of Abraham, who, upon his wife's instructions and in the face of God's promise that Sarah would give birth to a son, took his wife's handmaid, had sexual intercourse with her, and reproduced a child with her.

Furthermore, it is clear from the biblical accounts that God protected both Hagar and Ishmael, and He blessed Ishmael despite the fact he was not the covenant child and was instead, the product of an extramarital relationship. God also subsequently fulfilled His promise to Abraham and Sarah, despite their own decision to assist God and hasten His promise. Both would also later reproduce a son—the covenant child, whose name was Isaac.

From the scriptural accounts, we further observe that Isaac married Rebekah. Rebekah was Isaac's only wife and reproduction partner; so Isaac, in a departure from his father's footprints, reverted to the fulfillment of the original intention of the marital union as created by God. The union of Isaac and Rebekah reproduced twin sons, Jacob and Esau. In Jacob, we see the continuation of polygyny by the taking of both Leah and Rachel as his wives (although it was his original intention to only marry Rachel). This was with the agreement and approval of their father, Laban, who was also Jacob's uncle. Here again, we see no scriptural evidence that this polygamous behavior was condemned by God or the society of that era.

There is solid evidence to support Sarah's view that it was permissible for Abraham to reproduce with Hagar. In Sarah's case, Hagar was her property to command as she pleased. In biblical times, women were considered property and men were their masters. Prior to marriage, their fathers ruled over them, and after marriage, their husbands did. A handmaid was still a lower level of property of women than a wife, and in such a case, the wife was in control of the handmaid. This is why Hagar had no say in whether she would have sexual relations with Abraham. Sarah could do with her as she pleased. Abraham bore this out when he told Sarah (who later began to complain to him about Hagar during Hagar's pregnancy) that Hagar was *her* maidservant and she should do to Hagar what she thought was best.

There is also solid evidence to support Laban's view that it was acceptable for Jacob to marry both of his daughters in exchange for fourteen years of consecutive service from Jacob to him. The only thing Laban required was that Jacob pay the bride-price (dowry) for Rachel as well as Leah. We can only assume, based on this evidence, that the actions by biblical characters and their acceptance of polygamous practice were informed by a combination of their spiritual beliefs of what was right (nonsinful) and wrong (sinful) behavior and acceptable societal norms and customs.

There are those who might still question whether Lamech, Sarah, Abraham, Hagar, Jacob, Leah, Rachel, and Laban were under God's law at the time of these events, as the Ten Commandments and other laws forbidding adultery and other sexual sins were only pronounced in the Exodus of the Israelites from Egypt (and long after these earlier events). However, one can also find authority supporting the views I put forward above in Exodus 22:16–17. The law as given to Moses by God provided that if a man seduced a virgin who was not engaged, and lay with her, he must pay the customary bride-price for her to be his wife. If her father absolutely refused to give her to him, he must still pay money equal to the dowry for virgins. In this example again, there is no punishment for the man and woman having sexual intercourse. Furthermore, there is no absolute requirement that a marriage must follow. The only punishment is for the man, and it is the increase in the value of the bride-price, this being paid to the father whether the father gave the woman to the man to marry or not. Therefore, the man in this situation could have paid out a vast amount of money for a woman that he might never be given as his wife.

While the passage does not support any views that this behavior might amount to fornication (whether in the biblical or modern sense), the passage is relevant in its illustration that sexual violations against women were deemed as wrong because women were property. To violate a woman in this way was a dishonor to the person who was in charge of her (e.g., her father).

The passage also addresses another important piece of the monogamy/infidelity dialogue. It deals directly with premarital sex, another controversial and arguably unsettled topic in Christendom. A full treatment of that topic is outside the scope of this book, but we will address the issue in some detail as this chapter progresses. While every case of polygamy would need to be examined on its own facts, we can certainly assume that as the Bible does not record any disapproval or denunciation by God of the practice of polygamy in the above situations, God did not frown angrily upon the practice of polygamy.

We can go on and on about various men from biblical times who were engaged in polygamous relationships. However, the practice of polygamy in Bible times is perhaps most clearly seen through the

The Monogamy Mystery

stories of David, a man whom God Himself described as a man after His own heart; and David's son, Solomon, a man whom God declared the wisest man who would ever live.

Of importance to the issue of monogamy as it concerns David and Solomon is a commandment God gave to the Israelite kings. The Lord commanded the kings of Israel against taking *many* wives so that their hearts would not be led astray (Deuteronomy 17:17). The *Oxford English Dictionary* defines the word *many* as "a large number; numerous; countless; innumerable." The same dictionary defines the word *several* as meaning more than two, but not many; a few; some.

The Bible records that David had six wives and several concubines. Based on the above dictionary definitions and assuming that modern definitions of these words are consistent with the definitions of the words used in biblical times, I would think that David probably did not violate God's commands in this regard. It is also important to understand that the introduction of concubines also makes it clear that a man was allowed to have sexual relations with other women whom he was not married to, but who were his property.

A concubine was a female who was not of a class that qualified her to marry her master but who voluntarily enslaved herself to her master for his sexual pleasure. She did not have equal status with a wife. Although she was fully aware that her master had wives and that her relationship with him was not exclusive for him, she understood that her relationship with her master was exclusive for her. The more powerful a man was in those times, the more wives and concubines he was likely to have.

Some of these concubines were gifts for winning battles when nations went to war. It is to be noted that due to the way societies were ordered in biblical times, these men and women would not have believed that they were doing anything wrong, and their behavior does not appear to have been castigated as wrong or sinful by God or the society of that era.

A woman on the other hand, was not allowed to behave as the men were allowed; to do so would violate the property and sexual rights her husband had over her as his property. It is the reason that in biblical times, adultery was not only a sin, for the woman, it was also a criminal offence punishable by death (by stoning) according to the law of Moses. The notion of women from biblical times being considered as property rights also explains how much earlier women were being socialized differently than men as it relates to acceptable sexual behavior.

Of course, in today's society, those biblical conditions for acquiring wives and concubines would not work as they did then. This is so for two main reasons: today's women have the same sexual freedoms as men, which was not the case in biblical times, and women are no longer considered property. In most societies, women can choose whom they wish to have casual sex with and whom they wish to marry. They therefore cannot be won at auctions and as war prizes or be given in marriage without their consent (with some exceptions) in most present-day countries—not legally at least.

The point I wish to emphasize here is that there is no evidence (subject to the rules established for the kings of Israel) that God ever condemned a man who married more than one wife or who acquired concubines as property, perhaps based on his military rank, social status, power, and wealth. I believe that if societies were ordered in this way today, this position would also pertain. However, we are not so ordered, and different considerations have become relevant.

Solomon continued this tradition of polygamy (albeit on a grandiose scale) after succeeding his father, David, to the throne of Israel. Solomon is recorded to have had seven hundred wives of royal birth and three hundred concubines. Based on the *Oxford* definitions above of the terms *many* and *several*, I would say that Solomon violated the command God gave against kings of Israel taking many wives.

As we know, both David and Solomon were mighty men who were abundantly blessed and strategically used by God. They had huge and ambitious mandates and agendas in fulfilling the requirements for God's chosen people during their reign as kings of Israel. Yet, there is consistency with earlier periods in the Bible in that the general practice of polygamy by David and Solomon never seemed to raise God's eyebrows. In fact, despite the several wives and concubines David had, the only aspect of David's polygamous life that appeared to have caught God's attention was when he slept with Bathsheba, the wife of Uriah, the Hittite.

Bathsheba was David's most famous wife due to the circumstances in which she became his wife. As the biblical account illustrates, while Uriah was out to war, fighting on Israel's behalf, David encountered Bathsheba in all her radiance and beauty (while she was bathing). As the king, he requested her presence, engaged in extramarital sex with her, and she became impregnated in the process. David's polygamous action raised a red flag with God, as his actions constituted adultery in God's eyes. David did not simply marry another wife or casually add another unmarried woman as a concubine. He did not just have sex with his wife's handmaid as Abraham had done. He had sex with another man's wife and caused a grave injustice to that man in the process.

The story presents a clear illustration of God's view of adultery. It demonstrates that God will not simply wink at adultery. The obligation against the coveting of another person's wife is one of the Ten Commandments, which God gave to Moses for the people of Israel to follow. We might therefore surmise that in all the previous examples of polygamy discussed above, there was no censure by God because the polygamy was not perceived as adultery.

In the case of David and Bathsheba, however, David was obviously in violation of a divine principle that God had on marriage, which prohibited a man from taking the wife of another man. So God judged David's decision and actions with harsh and generational consequences. The judgment God pronounced on David in 2 Samuel 12:7–14 was along the following lines (taken from the KJV, NIV, and MSG versions of the Bible, combined and paraphrased for added emphasis):

> Because you have despised me and took the wife of Uriah, the Hittite as your wife, the sword shall not depart from thine house [killing and murder will continually plague your family]. I'll make trouble for you and bring calamity upon you out of your own family. Adversity will come against you from your own house. I'll take your wives from right out in front of you and I'll give them to your neighbor [someone close to you] and he will go to bed with them openly [in broad daylight]. You did your deed in secret. I'm doing mine in broad daylight with the whole country [Israel] watching. Because by this deed you have given the enemies of the Lord great occasion to blaspheme, the child born to you shall surely die.

We can easily compare this judgment to God's response to Abraham and Sarah's situation. God protected Hagar and Ishmael. Ishmael lived, but the child born to David and Bathsheba died. David's house was cursed, but Abraham's house was blessed. Both Ishmael and Isaac were blessed according to God's desire, but David and Bathsheba sorrowed and mourned over the death of their firstborn child.

Why the obvious difference in treatment? Could it perhaps be that David made a conscious decision to have sex with the wife of another man (Uriah), violated the rights Uriah had to his wife, caused a grave injustice to Uriah, and therefore sinned in God's view, while Abraham simply had sex with his wife's handmaid (an unmarried woman, who was his wife's property) and did not sin?

Further, as regards Solomon, although it appears that he violated God's commands in terms of marrying many wives, it does not seem that the marrying of the wives itself was God's main issue. His main issue appeared to be the fact that Solomon's heart would be led astray from Him. On the one hand, God was perhaps of the view that due to the high level of responsibility that leaders such as kings had in biblical times, they should not be distracted with the added responsibility and the wild pleasures associated with keeping many wives and concubines. Kings of nations in biblical times were not ceremonial positions. They were the actual leaders and decision makers and were often on the front line of battle when nations went to war. They therefore needed to be of a clear and uncluttered mind in leading God's people during those difficult periods.

On the other hand, God was also concerned as to the nationality of these wives and warned against the taking of foreign wives because these women would lead the kings of Israel astray to worship other gods. This is fundamental because God had been adamant and consistent as to how jealous He was as it concerned other gods competing with Him.

As the story records, Solomon loved many foreign women and took them as wives. He held fast to them in love, and they turned his heart from God toward other gods, and he did evil in the eyes of the Lord. He built high places for incense to be burned and sacrifices to be offered to these foreign gods against the commandments of the Lord. It appears that it was his following other gods that caught God's attention and not the polygamous behavior itself. God's punishment for Solomon's idolatrous actions (and not his polygamy) was to tear the entire kingdom away from him, save for one tribe that God left with him (not for his sake but for David's sake), and to give it to one of his subordinates.

John I. Cline

Did God relax His standards on male/female relationships and allow biblical society to operate in these polygamous relationships (adultery excepted) with impunity? Did God chose who He permitted to commit "adultery" with impunity and who He would punish if they did commit the "ultimate sin"?

Biblical scholars have several theories as to why polygamy appeared to have been accepted in biblical society. The theory most accepted has to do with the disparity in the male and female population and its causes. The theory proposes that historically there has always been an imbalance between the male and female population with women accounting for more of the population than men. One factor that was a major contributor to this disparity was that during ancient times men went to war while the women stayed at home. Wars during these times were brutal, with a high rate of fatality, and over time, there were fewer men available for women of ancient times to marry.

There is evidence to support another reason for this imbalance in the human population. Historically, women enjoyed a longer lifespan than men, and this also contributed to the number of women who remained available and in need of male commitment. Further, in these ancient societies, which were controlled by men, women did not provide for themselves. Since in those times the traditional role of a woman was more one of support to her male husband and as the nurturing and nonfinancial caretaker of the family unit, women were uneducated, untrained, and dependent on a male-led household for survival. This significant ratio of women to men in the population and the emphasis on role-playing by both men and women in society left many women in a less-than-desirable position. Biblical men would then be justified in taking multiple wives in order to support and protect these women.

Still, it may be the theory of other biblical scholars that the struggle of mankind with monogamy is inextricably linked to the fall of man (through Adam's original sin), as once Adam sinned, the covenant and all the laws of God went out the window, so to speak. This means that although polygamy was not God's standard, monogamy was an existence that man in his fallen state would be expected to struggle with.

These scholars reiterate, however, that in the beginning, it was not so. In the beginning, God's Word declared that a man should leave his father and mother and cleave to his wife (not wives) and that the two (not three or four) shall become one flesh. Therefore, one husband to one wife is God's standard, and we should continue to strive to achieve God's standards, even in our fallen state.

While all the above views may hold true, my view is much simpler and direct. In my view, it does not appear from the many cases examined that in every case where God's intended standard for marriage is not met due to some decision or action taken, He would consider the decision/action as sinful. If we believe that God is all knowing and never changing, then His standards do not change due to population imbalances, social circumstances, and spiritual decay, as these events would have been contemplated by Him in His infinite wisdom before He laid the foundations of the world. Hence, what He deems to be a sin and what He deems not to be a sin will be consistent throughout time.

As hard as this may be for the church to swallow, in an open-minded, proper analysis of biblical Scriptures and contrary to our thousands of years of preaching, it does not appear that in God's eyes all premarital sex amounted to sin. There is no clear scriptural authority that all sexual intercourse occur only between legally married people; it does not appear that a man having many wives amounted to adultery; nor does it appear that a man marrying/having many wives, and at the same time having sex with his various concubines, amounted to the sins of fornication or adultery.

In fact, God told David's prophet, Nathan, in pronouncing David's judgment, that if all He gave David (including all the wives of Saul—David's master), and all of Judah and Israel), was not enough for him, He would have given him more of those things (see 2 Samuel 12:8). Moreover, it should be noted that when God gave Saul's wives to David, David was already a married man. Why would He have done that if He considered the practice of polygamy to be sinful? What is abundantly clear from Scripture is that God has been consistent that having sex with the spouse of another man or woman is wrong, and this is what He considers as adultery. King Solomon appears to have understood this all too well. In distinguishing between a thief and a murderer, he says in Proverbs 6:32 (NIV), "But a man who commits adultery, lacks wisdom [has no sense] and he corrupts [destroys] his own soul."

Admittedly, I have come to the above conclusions Old Testament style and have perhaps not convinced the New Testament philosophers along the path. There are those who would argue that although the Old Testament did not have authority condemning this polygamous practice, the New Testament Scriptures on sex and sexual immorality point in the opposite direction and it is those Scriptures that we should rely upon as Christians following the resurrected Christ.

I do agree with the principle of this view, but I do not believe that the problem emanates from a conflict between Old Testament authority and New Testament authority. Although the type of behavior that was unacceptable in biblical times was consistent in both the

Old and New Testaments, the reason there appears to be two different standards on polygamy in the Old and New Testaments seems to be due to a translation of Greek terminology to other languages such as English.

Many biblical scholars have taken the time to research and comment on this issue and a full treatment of the discussion is outside the scope of this book.

The conclusion seems to be that there is sufficient evidence to demonstrate that fornication referenced in the 1 Corinthians 7 context was never intended to be extended to all acts of premarital or extramarital sex. In biblical societies, women were not legally and culturally allowed to have casual sex with men prior to marriage as it is today. Such action would be legally punished. They were the property of their fathers or other legal guardians, and they were betrothed for a price. Therefore biblical men had two choices: either to choose these women as wives in order to have sexual relations with them, or resort to other types of women (prostitutes) who could be bought at perhaps a cheaper price, simply for sex and without the extra commitment of having to take them as a wife.

Because women were considered property and had no decision-making power, there was no option three (as there is today)—that is for men to choose women who were not regarded as prostitutes but who would have sexual relations as part and parcel of an interpersonal relationship and without a marriage commitment. This "option" was never considered in Scripture due to the different nature of biblical societies.

Paul's instructions to the church at Corinth therefore became necessary as men were by the time of Paul resorting to the latter (prostitution) as opposed to marrying (which was God's original intention based on Old Testament authority in Genesis 1). This was the mischief that Paul sought to address in 1 Corinthians 7, and in so doing, reconciled with Old Testament authority in this regard. In leaving this point, it is my view that while we are biblically clear that having sex with the spouse of another man or woman constitutes adultery, it does not appear that there is any clear biblical authority on whether fornication extends to all sexual relations outside of marriage. The word was translated to a modern society that it was never developed for or within, and whose culture and customs are much different than the society in which the concept was applied. It is therefore the reason many theologians have concluded that the Bible gives us no clear scriptural insistence that all sexual intercourse must occur only between married people or that polygamy is a sin.

I hope that this explanation suffices to link the bridge that my views left open between the Old Testament and New Testament authorities on polygamous behavior (adultery and fornication). I will revisit the issue a final time and conclude my views on it in chapter 9 when I discuss the role of spirituality. To answer a question raised earlier, I do believe that biblical authority should be spiritual authority, provided that when relying on biblical authority, it is properly understood in its context.

In exiting this perhaps controversial but foundational chapter, I reemphasize that no matter how much we discuss the symptoms and causes of polygamy, attempt to denounce or condemn polygamy and celebrate and/or encourage monogamy, it does not lessen the impact of polygamous behavior in interpersonal relationships and the challenges of being monogamous in today's society (regardless of one's ethnicity, culture, gender, sexual orientation, or religious persuasion). The reality of all of our existence is that people wrestle with a monogamous way of life (while perhaps paying lip service to the theory of monogamy as ideal).

Yet, so alarming are the consequences of polygamy to those ordering our society that different societies and religious sects have sought different ways to mitigate these consequences. The African Muslims have legislated in favor of polygamy, so that in these jurisdictions, the practice of having multiple wives has been legalized. On the contrary, the Muslims of the Far East, with certain exceptions (e.g., the sheiks who can have multiple wives), have legislated against it with penalties for breach of legislation, resulting in death. Christian societies have also legislated in favor of monogamy, albeit with less harsh penalties than those of the Far East Muslim societies, but Christian churches preach vehemently against any form or variation of polygamy.

Nevertheless, in all of these religious, societal, or cultural circles in which the principle of monogamy is regarded as too important or valuable to be interfered with, polygamous behavior remains the single most common and persisting threat to marital relationships, the most significant challenge for men and women in committed relationships, and a critical undermining factor to the institution of the family in the greater society.

It is the very reason I raised the question earlier: Were we really designed to be monogamous? We will respond to this question head-on in the next chapter.

CHAPTER 2
Is Biology to Blame?

Is there a biological basis for monogamous behavior? Is monogamy caused by our biology? Whether the biological makeup of human beings is responsible for the inability of most humans to remain monogamous is a critical issue to resolve. The issue becomes critical since it is assumed that most people aspire to be happy, and the pursuit of individual aspects of this happiness includes having successful interpersonal relationships.

As human beings, we meet people with whom we fall in love and/or we love deeply, and the majority of us want nothing more than to ensure that they are happy being in relationship with us. Yet, we struggle with the number one cause of relationship breakups: infidelity. Infidelity is a type of polygamous behavior that operates as an epidemic for which no societal institution seems to have a cure. The epidemic has been identified in society, but it does not appear to have been properly examined.

Unfortunately, for us humans, the consequences of this societal ill is glaringly evident, repetitive, and very present due to the absence of proper treatment. It is therefore important for us to determine the cause of non-monogamous behavior so that we can identify a treatment for the symptoms and bring about a more achievable solution for society as a whole.

John I. Cline

All mammals have one common foundation: a biological structure. According to some studies, only 10 to 15 percent of all primate species are monogamous, and less than 3 percent of mammals are monogamous. Biologists seem to agree on the view that birds are the most monogamous animals in the world—much more so than humans or any other animal. Ninety percent of bird species pair up exclusively to mate and rear their young together. In regard to the animal kingdom, it is reported that only in the range of 3 to 5 percent of the four thousand mammalian species practice monogamy, having only one mate. These mammals include wolves, mole rats, beavers, and meerkats.

The gray wolf, for example, has been observed as being generally monogamous, as they are concerned mostly with the pedigree of the offspring these wolves seek to reproduce. To achieve this, the two wolves qualifying as the dominant pair (the alpha pair) in a gray wolf pack are the only two members of the pack that breed. The mated pair usually remains together for life, unless one of the pair dies. With the death of an alpha wolf, a new alpha male or female will usually emerge and take over as the mate of the surviving wolf, so that the most dominant wolves continue to mate in order to continue to reproduce gray wolves of the highest pedigree.

There is therefore very little support for monogamous behavior among mammals. Moreover, as it pertains to the human mammal, left to the natural order of life without social or spiritual teaching or influence, the evidence suggests that this same lack of support holds true across all cultures and races. The conclusion appears to be that the only natural force affecting the behavior of animals is their biology.

On the other hand, a human animal that has been placed within a social structure tells a completely different story. Within such a structure, several factors influence the tendency to strive for monogamy. These include sociology, psychology, anthropology, economics, and law—all of which we will examine in some detail in the next chapter.

Although the biological makeup of animals has been identified as the primary reason for sexual behavior in animals, scientists have yet to conclude that a gene or hormone really exists that makes a man or woman monogamous. The Proceedings of the National Academy of Sciences in the USA have published a study that seems to suggest that a particular hormone found in humans as well as other mammals plays an important role in encouraging monogamy. The suggestion appears to be more conclusive as it pertains to males than females and indicates that where the particular hormone is stronger in males, the bond with their female partners is strong, and where the hormone is weak, the bond with their female partners is also weak. Where the bond is weak, quite naturally, the males feel unsatisfied with and/or cheat on their partners.

Over a number of years in researching the hormone, vasopressin, the study has examined a gene for vasopressin in the human brain. Based on testing, a particular variation of the gene, which is called "allele 334," was associated with lower scores on partner bonding and greater odds of marital conflict. This effect was concentrated in men.

The study showed for example, that among men who had little or no trace of the allele 334 gene, a lower percentage (15 to 16 percent) reported marital crisis; and in men who had two copies of the allele 334 gene, the odds of marital crisis doubled to approximately 34 percent. Is infidelity then a genetic problem?

The hormone oxytocin has also been identified as a hormone that might make men monogamous—well, almost! Oxytocin is referred to as the "trust hormone" or the "love molecule." It is typically associated with helping couples establish a greater sense of intimacy and attachment and is believed to be highly critical in human pair bonding. Scientific studies have indicated that this hormone accounts for the reason some people are unfaithful and why some husbands are more faithful than others. It appears to be the chemical in the blood of humans and the brain that creates bonds of trust in relationships.

In a study by the Proceedings of the National Academy of Sciences in the USA, forty young men (all of whom had been in a relationship for at least six months and reported being passionately in love with their partners) were placed in a brain scanner. These men had either inhaled oxytocin or placebo via nasal spray while they viewed photos of either their partners, women they knew but were not dating, and women they had never met but who were equally as attractive as the partners of the men.

The study showed that the pleasure and desire regions of the brains of the men who were given the oxytocin hormone lit up when they saw photographs of women they loved, but not when they looked at total strangers. Some of the pleasure regions were also activated by images of women the men knew, but not as strongly as these areas lit up by the photographs of their loved ones.

While the men who were given oxytocin in the study had a strong reaction to those women with whom they were in love, the study does not suggest that these men were or remained monogamous to their partners. In fact, even if this fact could be established, these men do not represent the majority in society. The question still remains unanswered as to whether genetics is a handicap to being monogamous.

We have all been on our own personal journey, trying to understand the dynamics of our interpersonal relationships. Many have written books and articles on the topic. Others have sung songs about sex and love. The song "What's Love Got to Do with It," made popular by Tina Turner, is instructive here. It speaks to the natural response by a woman to the physical touch of a man as opposed to a response to the specific touch of someone with whom one is in a committed relationship.

The lyrics of the first verse of the song begin this way: "You must understand why the touch of your hand makes my pulse react. It's only the thrill of boy meeting girl, opposites attract." Therefore, the song tends to align with the biology of humans in suggesting that if the conditions are right (whether it be a random connection at a bar; a planned candlelight dinner; a determined intention; or an emotionally charged response to a situation), it is those conditions that would be the determining factors as to whether these persons engage in intimate, sexual relations.

Hence, it is not unusual or unnatural once two persons get close enough to each other and these persons can connect, that the bodies will respond and the brain will begin to release the endorphin hormone. In such cases, love, commitment, or marriage play no role in the decision to engage sexually/intimately. Unfortunately, this natural response is not as a result of finding the right person or being in a committed relationship or a marriage. It is a biological phenomenon, or in the words of the writer of the song, "What's Love Got to Do with It": "It's physical, only logical. You must try to ignore that it means more than that"!

Therefore, we can safely agree that sexual arousal is biological, and sexual pleasure is perhaps the highest of all human pleasures. For most, if not all humans, nothing we do gives us greater stimulation and satisfaction than sexual intimacy. In those intimate moments, the feeling is as though the sexual pleasure is a consequential reward from God of heightened sensuality and intensive climax packaged within the procreation process. It's a feeling we desire over and over again as humans, especially in our youth, when we are healthier, stronger, more attractive, and our sexual appetite is at an all-time high.

If there is no moral or spiritual code to inform or order this natural desire (that gives us such heightened pleasure and ecstasy), all humans will randomly seek to have sexual intimacy as often as they can with whomever they can. It is just the nature of man at its best, acting to fulfill the basic human need of sexual intimacy and fulfill the natural human purpose of procreation. It finds its place in humans around the age of puberty as a necessary stage in human biological development.

For example, usually between the ages of twelve to fourteen (when they hit puberty), boys will experience sexual arousal, which will then propel some or most boys to want to masturbate, since at this young age there is, in the majority of cases, no identified sexual partner, love, or commitment to anyone of the opposite sex. If we then stretch this conclusion to its most possible limits, the natural experience of being sexually aroused is not limited to one person at any given time or over a period of time. Humans may be physically attracted to more than one person at a time and may be sexually aroused by and sexually arouse more than one person at a time, irrespective of whether such persons are in committed relationships with each other.

Therefore, we can conclude in agreeing with the many studies in this area that it is not natural (supported by biology) for persons to exhibit continuous and uninterrupted monogamous behavior. The natural, biological structure of animals, including humans, tends to suggest a desire for sexual/intimate connections based on physical factors only. It is very possible that acceptance of this conclusion provides the starting point for finding the solution for infidelity in society.

The simple diagnosis appears to be that humans are not biologically designed to practice monogamy successfully. Instead, they were designed to respond to physical stimuli, whether or not they are in an exclusive and committed relationship filled with love. One sensible question that could be asked then is whether it was sensible for those ordering our society to do so in disregard of our collective biological blueprint.

On the assumption that we have located the problem surrounding monogamy in society, we should also now determine if we can identify the solution. In seeking to do this, we need to look at the course that infidelity has taken and its outcomes, as well as the possibility or likelihood of recovery from the "no or low tolerance for monogamy" mentality in our society. It is certainly easy to believe that those who ordered our society recognized the problem very early on, and in recognition of these consequences then sought to invoke other factors as a justification for monogamy, despite the natural, biological tendencies. Two major factors that I will examine in later chapters are the roles of sociology and spirituality in ordering society based on the tenets of monogamy.

CHAPTER 3
The Sociology of Monogamy

If it is accepted that biology is a plausible cause for the inability to maintain a mostly monogamous society, it must then also be determined why society places a premium on monogamy and how sociology plays a role in the argument in favor of monogamy. Sociology is the study of society and its origin, structure, and development, while anthropology (closely related) has to do with the study of humans, past and present, especially human culture and development. In tracing our own development as a society over time, it is a valid point to underscore that while monogamy may not be natural, there is a strong argument for its desirability.

In fact, there are many things we do as humans that are desirable, although they are not natural. For example, we do not naturally know how to read, but learning to read is desirable in order to be literate in our society. Neither did Michael Phelps, USA Olympic swimmer and multi-gold medalist, naturally know how to swim, nor is gymnastics a natural, physical reaction for Gabrielle Douglas, USA Olympic gymnast and gold medalist. However, each of these developed talents has its advantages, and each has been the catalyst of a much decorated life for Michael and Gabby.

So too society has been socialized to accept monogamy. The state of maintaining monogamy might then be viewed as a learned skill, an acquired taste. Its importance has been emphasized by the drafters of society who believed that the advantages of monogamy are worth the costs of a monogamous socialization.

Social monogamy (marriage to one person and the encouragement to reproduce within a marriage) was thought to be one solution to the polygamy/infidelity problem in society. In societies that uphold the principle of monogamy as sacrosanct, the institution of marriage to one person is paramount. In these societies, laws were developed around this ideal, and monogamy has been postulated to be so vital to the thriving of these societies that marriage to more than one person is dealt with by law and is a crime punishable by imprisonment.

Literature has also been developed around this platform, and we teach it to our children as a means of reiterating the concept and renewing the psychology underpinning monogamy. Our social circumstances, the laws that regulate our society, and the relating literature (e.g., the definition of *fornication* we examined in chapter 1), therefore inform our psychology. We are programmed to behave in a certain way in order to be accepted by the society at large, notwithstanding the obvious individual struggles we have when our psychology is in conflict with our biology.

Over time, we are socialized to understand and believe that only monogamous behavior is ethical. We are expected to inform our biology (so to speak) of this socialized belief so that it can learn to act accordingly. These ideals then form part and parcel of our understanding of morality and our ethical standards, and form our basis for judging others.

As one looks at the sociological and anthropological factors, it may be immediately realized that in ordering Western societies, the human animal was socialized to accept monogamy as the proper and most efficient way to live and rear and protect children. This theory is certainly justified in terms of economics, as it is certainly more economical to society to have single-family homes as opposed to a breadwinner having to provide for more than one family at a time. The crafters of organized societal living were also concerned with the charge that would be brought on society in situations where persons would be reproducing without the ability to financially support their children—a concern that monogamy was also intended to address.

As an anecdote, most of these societies are structured from a biblically informed perspective as well, notwithstanding the acceptance of the theory of segregation of church and state. This theory is enshrined in the constitution (which is the supreme law of the land in every country). However, these societies would perhaps prefer to justify their sociological norms on a sense of what seems right, wrong, moral or immoral to a reasonable mind, as opposed to biblical principles. On the contrary, other societies that encourage polygamy, polygyny, and polyandry (another form of polygamy—one woman and multiple men) have taught a different psychology than that of the Western world. Such societies socialize their people according to the acceptance of polygamous behavior and create literature in order to reinforce the psychology of the legality of polygamy in society. The laws are therefore drafted in order to legalize polygamy so that it is not punishable by law. In these societies, there may be recognition of this natural biology that we cannot deny. At the very least, there is recognition that a person can have a successful family life with more than one spouse. Economics is also a factor in these societies, as a person would need to be of a certain financial stature in order to have more than one spouse, since it is a legal requirement that the spouses be taken care of to a certain prescribed standard.

From a theoretical perspective, Western societies holding monogamy as trite, have developed and implemented the legal infrastructure required to promote and encourage monogamy. The question is whether this initiative has transcended to the other aspects of societal living. It requires examination as to whether individuals living in these societies have been socialized in order to live monogamous lives according to the way in which monogamous societies have been legally structured. To do so, we need to examine whether the dating infrastructure in these societies is supportive of the legal infrastructure. The examination can commence from the beginning of our dating lives.

In Western societies, young men have traditionally been allowed and encouraged to date and carry on intimate relationships with multiple women at the same time in order to ensure that they have made an informed and intelligent decision as to who they intend to spend the rest of their lives with. While it is readily acceptable for a man to date more than one woman in an effort to weed out others and choose one, the same mentality does not hold true for the woman. In most societies, it is almost glorified for a man to be of interest to many women who are all willing to date him at the same time with the intention to compete for that ultimate spot in his life; whereas a woman who has the same ability and acts upon it would not be considered chaste or ladylike.

Here again, there is an obvious double standard at play in the way men are typically allowed, and women are usually expected to date in Western cultures. The different treatment and expectations between men and women during the dating stage also presents a disconnect between men and women in committed relationships, as the ideal expected behavior from men within a marriage is diametrically opposed to the encouraged behavior for men in the dating stage in preparing them for marriage. The sociological rites of passage we refer to as dating do not serve to encourage the idea of monogamy even though a monogamously functioning society is set as our ideal.

More recently in these Western societies, television programs such as *The Bachelor* and *The Bachelorette* have further influenced the mentality behind dating. The literature presented on these television programs demonstrates an equaling of the dating infrastructure for men and women. These programs promote the idea of one person dating multiple partners at the same time in an effort to determine who would be the ultimate winner of "the bachelor" or "the bachelorette" in that particular season.

These dating arrangements very frequently transform into relationships (pre-marriage) of a more committed form, where relationships are continuously carried on with one man and multiple female partners or one woman and multiple male partners. Having been socialized in this polygamous way (with most or all of these relationships being intimate, filled with sexual contact, and encouraged by televised literature, family, and friends), men and women are then expected to one day find a mate, hold solely to that one mate, and behave monogamously for the rest of their natural lives.

The fundamental drawback with this approach is the well-settled view that human beings are creatures of habit. So the dating process presents a contradiction to both men and women as it relates to their desired, socially or spiritually (as applicable) informed goal to be in a monogamous relationship.

Dating in Western societies, unfortunately, appears to be a double-edged sword. It is intended to be a weeding process but has also proven to be the seminal seed of a habit-forming behavior of continuously desiring multiple partners throughout one's life (especially in men). This is so, since the desire to be with multiple men or women does not extinguish simply upon a particular mate being chosen or winning the "beauty contest" in order for both parties to facilitate a legal structure that the particular society will accept. This habit, coupled with the challenges of the biological structure of humans examined in the previous chapter, only serves to exacerbate the monogamy problem in our society.

Alternatively, in cultures where monogamy plays a more visible and major part of their spiritual and social value system, dating is very different. Marriage is approached from a societal and family perspective and is not an individualistic decision-making process. In these societies, the entire family is involved in the dating process. There is little or no physical contact and no sexual contact prior to marriage. Sexual involvement is reserved specifically for marriage. This is particularly true, for example, in certain Hindu cultures, where parental involvement is mandatory both in terms of the choice of a mate, and also the courtship and post-wedding familiarization and integration process.

As an illustration, I have an Indian friend who was also an ex-coworker of mine. When his father called him, indicating to him that they had found him a bride, he left the island of Tortola in the British Virgin Islands and went back to India to meet his wife for the first time. He subsequently married the chosen bride. In our discussions about the selection process and the next steps in the marriage, he explained to me that for a year after he was married to his wife, the new bride would be required to live with his parents. During that time, she would be taught and introduced to the ways in which he was raised, the type of foods he was used to eating and how to prepare such foods, as well as other practices to which he was accustomed.

In this example, we see a complete societal attempt at promoting monogamy and the importance of the institution of marriage, a value that is held highly in Hindu societies. It is an important value that is not simply encouraged in theory but is supported by an infrastructure in which the entire society has a role.

While some studies indicate that Indian men can be as unfaithful as any other man, so that such societal support systems may not guarantee the maintenance of continuous monogamy within a marriage, polygamous behavior in these societies appears to be more controlled as the presence of it does not appear to break down these marriages irretrievably. Marriages in such societies survive longer, children are raised in double-parent homes, and the divorce rate is significantly lower than in Western civilization.

If we want to live and promote monogamy in Western societies as a social value, then the expectations of the training ground we refer to as the dating process must be equal for both men and women, and we all must hold each other accountable for behaving in a way that is consistent with our values and value system in this regard. The entire society must buy into this value system, and the literature (e.g., television programs) would also need to be redirected and recast in order to sensitize current and future generations regarding the importance of monogamy.

The promotion and success of the monogamy model in society is in no way possible without a concerted effort on the part of our society (socially, religiously, and otherwise) to develop the requisite supporting social infrastructure, train up our children by teaching them these social values as core values, and demonstrate and reinforce these core values through the social infrastructure. This shift would go a long way in strengthening the family unit, and the society would then be strengthened as a result of its substratum (the family) being strengthened.

CHAPTER 4
Infidelity in Society

Men and women deal with real-life challenges associated with infidelity, whether married or unmarried, religious or nonreligious, Christian or non-Christian. Recent global statistics show that approximately 70 percent of men admit to having had an affair and, perhaps surprisingly to some, women were not too far behind in admitting to having had an affair (50 to 60 percent). Further, these percentages are greater for the unmarried, non-Christian, and nonreligious demographics.

In reality though, it might appear that a larger number of men commit adultery than women. There is also biblical authority supporting the view that sexual temptation is greater for men than for women, as Matthew 5:28 hints exclusively to men lusting after women and committing adultery in their hearts. However, women struggle likewise with sexual temptations, and as the statistics bear out— to a significant degree as well. In fact, I was in a conversation with a young lady once who was aware that her father was unfaithful to her mother and had relationships with multiple women at a time. She later admitted to me that based on certain events that had taken place in her life on the same night with several different men, that she was absolutely convinced that she could be just like her father. I also personally know of several other women who have carried on relationships with multiple men while in a primary committed relationship.

John I. Cline

Over my twenty plus years of pastoral counseling, I have counseled many ordinary, good men and women, husbands and wives who found themselves dealing with the issue of infidelity. These men and women did not have a willful or conscious predisposition for being promiscuous or irresponsible, but they nevertheless found themselves in a situation that threatened their marriage, relationship, and/or family life.

Some may find it more alarming to learn that deacons, deaconesses, ministers, pastors, bishops, first ladies, prophets, and prophetesses (and the list of religious designations can go on) are not excluded from dealing with this very issue in their marriages as well. So too, these men and women of God are not inherently bad people, but they find themselves wrestling with a biological and natural pull or desire, coupled with a socialization that has not adequately prepared them for a monogamous existence. Hence, infidelity in Christendom has been a major contributor to pastors leaving their pulpits, to the breakdown or break up of churches, and to members leaving churches. It is also the cause of much discord among church members.

In almost none of these cases have I found anyone who embarked on their relationship with the calculated or premeditated mind-set of having an affair or not being monogamous. As a matter of fact, it is the erroneous belief of most people that marriage holds some magical cure for polygamous behavior. It certainly does not; and that kind of thinking and even preaching, where the unmarried are encouraged to marry in order to avoid "fornication" or to eliminate the temptation or risk of having multiple partners or "sleeping around" has not in most cases, proven beneficial and has been a disservice to those who have been so encouraged.

In my experience, during premarital counseling of couples, affairs were known of by one partner or the other, but the foreknowledge did not prevent them from proceeding to marriage with the hope that once married, the behavior would not recur. In most situations, this hope is never realized. Consequently, some people marry with false expectations as to what marriage is really intended to provide or cure in the existing relationship.

As a result, when the unwanted behavior does not change, there is much hurt, disappointment, pain, and frustration, which in a number of cases results in the breakdown of the marital relationship and which ultimately could end in divorce. While I will explore the issue in more detail in chapters 5 and 6, it gives me cause to pause and emphasize at this juncture that where someone has a propensity to be unfaithful in a relationship, marriage is definitely not the cure for such propensity.

I remember a particular couple in one of my premarital counseling sessions. The woman had knowledge that her intended husband was having an affair. She accepted his marriage proposal notwithstanding and was in effect communicating to the man that she accepted him as he was and regardless of the occurring infidelity. Even in circumstances where a man may have agreed with his intended wife that he would end an affair or has represented to her that the affair no longer exists, she must be very aware that just as a leopard cannot change its spots, so too is the likelihood very high that her intended may not change his behavior. So in having the capacity to agree to marry him in these circumstances, she must also have the capacity to love him through this fault.

When these post-marriage, monogamous expectations are not met, and the negative premarital behavior continues or resurfaces post marriage, not only does it affect the persons involved, but in a vast majority of cases, it will also affect any children who may have already been produced by the union. There is, however, hope for such a man, that his natural tendencies can change; that there is a force that can change his spots although he does not have the capacity to change them himself. We will explore this further in chapter 9.

In sharing my own realities with infidelity by way of example, I am a man who loves God and who loves fulfilling the call of God on my life as a bishop and a pastor. I love His people and I love His church. It was at the tender age of twelve, that I accepted the Lord as my personal Savior and became a Christian. As I began to grow spiritually, I also continued to grow physically, and naturally found that my attraction to the opposite sex was not limited to one woman.

As a Christian young man, I found myself dating multiple women at the same time. Of course, I was also taught and told repeatedly that sex outside of marriage was wrong. But all the God I had in me and all the teaching that I received from my church and my pastor somehow did not prevent me from naturally desiring and engaging in sex both within and outside of my committed relationships. It was soon clear to me that in spite of my love for God and ministry, I too had this thorn in my flesh and a proclivity to moral misappropriation in this area of my life. Further, I found that monogamy was uncommon among men, even Christian men.

At the age of twenty-five, I felt the call of God to ministry. I was licensed and ordained as a pastor in Bloomfield, New Jersey, shortly thereafter. At twenty-seven, I felt compelled to settle down and marry a wife because it was compatible with the teachings of the Bible and essential for my Christian living and ministry. I married a beautiful bride, who later bore me two sons. Now my life was filled with God, ministry, and family, but despite these three, I still found myself with wandering eyes and a subtle desire to yield to the many temptations that often presented themselves.

I preached holiness, and I counseled many young people to abstain from premarital sex, which counsel I still solidly believe in today. I knew the truth of God's Word concerning the sanctity of marriage and adultery. Nevertheless, I still found myself with the same struggle of remaining continuously faithful in my circumstances. It became even more alarming to me when I realized that in the realm of pastors or religious leaders, I was not alone in this struggle.

Over many years of pastoring from the pulpit and leading broken lives, witnessing failing pastors, trying to heal broken families, and seeking to mend discontented members, I decided to look further and not just rely on the various interpretations of biblical Scripture on fornication and adultery. I wanted to know not so much what I was restricted from doing, but what caused me to do what I was doing and wanted to do. I had to try to reconcile the patriarchs of the Old Testament with their many wives and concubines juxtaposed to the New Testament commands on sexual immorality, and I began my own journey. It is the compelling reason that I finally gathered the courage to record my findings in this book in hopes that they would serve, if nothing else, as a platform for discussion.

I am absolutely certain that the church has not adequately confronted this issue. It is my view that the church has only thrown Scriptures at it and preached at it without having dealt with or having a proper understanding of the biological cause and social effect on non-monogamous behavior. Whether the approach by the church is deliberate or simply a matter of ignorance can be debated, but it can no longer be tolerated as acceptable that non-monogamous behavior be simply ruled as a "sin" without further explanation relating to the root of the problem with monogamy.

I am also of the firm belief that many Christian pastors, and Christian men and women of the clergy share my view but would not voice their opinion on the issue publicly, since the truth may result in severe criticism of the bearer of it, could have severe consequences for society, and would challenge the hundreds of years of theological foundations that have been laid by the church.

In trying to fix the problem of infidelity, the effects of having set such standards without proper knowledge and understanding as to how to achieve fidelity have been far-reaching. Women who endeavor to uphold these standards find themselves, in many cases, wanting children but having no available candidates to procreate with and are therefore denied one of the greatest purposes of womanhood: childbearing and child rearing. Those women who do have children with men who are not "their own" are forced to keep it a secret, and the children often grow up without knowing their fathers or without the benefit of having their fathers participate in their upbringing, even when the fathers are known to the children.

The other unfortunate result of coping with infidelity in a monogamous society is that of abortion. Some women who have chosen not to have children (which is in contradistinction to their natural design to procreate) unless they have a husband, elect to take the abortive route. The more consequential sin I believe in all of this is when a child of infidelity is conceived, and in order to keep a secret or to protect the person involved due to societal pressure placed on women in this type of environment, many women resort to committing abortion.

Like David in his situation with Bathsheba, in seeking to rectify or cover up one sin (the pregnancy of Bathsheba), he committed another (killing the husband of the woman he had no right to, to begin with); so too, these women resort to abortion instead of having children outside of wedlock. The results of societal interference and insistence on this particular ideal seem to yield more consequences and fewer solutions to the problems.

It is my prayer that as Christian readers digest my findings, they will gain some holy boldness, put the consequences to one side, and begin to confront the real causes of infidelity that have caused the breakup of so many families, the low self-esteem in so many women and men, and the direct or indirect trauma caused to so many children.

CHAPTER 5
The Mystery of Infidelity

Having examined the foundational issues of monogamy and infidelity in the previous chapters, I hope that some of it has been demystified. Understanding the mystery could ease some of the hurt and restore some integrity to the broken lives resulting from this behavior. It is rarely the case that the spouse whose partner was unfaithful was not adequate enough, didn't make his or her partner happy or any of the other usual explanations offered as to why a person has been unfaithful. This human behavior is more deeply rooted and requires a more intelligent and open-minded conversation in order to find a real solution. For those willing to make the effort, there are solutions that can eliminate this behavior from the relationship.

The multimillion-dollar question that is asked is: Why do people cheat? Why would someone put the person he or she loves and promises to love through the agony, defeat, and rejection caused by an affair? At the beginning of a male/female relationship, attraction is prominent and usually the butterflies are present; then love is expressed. Devotion is pledged and eventually, in many cases at least, the vows are taken. All the desires of a love relationship are present and the longing to be in a committed, happy, long-term, lifetime relationship sets in. Everything we have seen in the movies and read about in the fairy tales suggest that once love has truly been found, then it is happily ever after!

Of course, the movies and fairy tales omit the nitty-gritty, and so as if out of nowhere, it feels like this foul and unwelcomed behavior just manifests in one of the parties in the relationship. Suddenly, all hopes and dreams seem to spiral out of control and in place of happiness, there is misery. In place of bliss, there is hurt. In place of love, there is resentment and confusion; and in place of contentment, there is discontent. Understanding does not come easy, and very little the offending partner can say at that moment will bring any level of clarity and healing to the emotional pain and fallout that have taken place in the relationship as a result of the infidelity.

The truth is that many people can explain *how* it happened, but they find difficulty in explaining *why* it happened. One of the reasons we never get to *why* is that in explaining behavior, men will try their utmost to first protect the emotions of their partner and the viability of the relationship. They do this because they have concluded that the partner can't handle the truth, and if she knew the truth, he would lose her and, where applicable, his family in the process.

Therefore, when men do admit to infidelity, getting to *why* is often lost in the explanation of *how*, and so the true reason is rarely ever discovered. The need to protect his partner's feelings is paramount for a man, but oftentimes, this would create more confusion in the woman's mind as she is usually blaming herself, assessing what could have been done better or what could be done differently in the future.

The woman is not so much interested in the *how*, but in the *why*. This presents an awkward situation that leaves many unanswered questions for the woman, and she is forced to push forward with her life (whether she chooses to continue in the particular relationship or not) in a confused emotional state. While some may view this approach as a cop-out, on analysis, it is really not.

It is inherent in the nature of man to provide and to protect. However, it is not inherent in his nature to discuss his true feelings, since to do so, he would have to become vulnerable and engage in conversation. As we know, these are two variables that are not endemic to most men. In this situation, most men become brick walls, and their true feelings would usually have to be extracted using various counseling methods. Where any of these true feelings, if expressed, would tend to hurt the woman he loves, then the *brick wall* phenomenon is exacerbated exponentially.

On the other hand, most women suffer greatly from the confession of their infidelity, and instead of being honest and confess the infidelity, they would try to cover it up. However, instead of going into protect mode as with the man, she goes into preservation mode in order to protect her integrity; her financial security; her own personal, physical, and emotional safety (i.e., avoiding physical, verbal, and emotional abuse); and where applicable, the stability of her children.

We often hear that women cheat as much or nearly as much as men, and statistics perhaps will also bear this out. We also often hear that men only appear to be more prolific cheaters because women are better at covering it up. That opinion may certainly be true as women tend to concentrate more on being thorough thinkers and analysts and will think a process through to the end. When the end is contemplated at the beginning, it is often easier to be more careful to avoid the exposure of the infidelity. It is the reason that in the majority of cases, a woman's infidelity is never exposed.

If she is forced to come full circle with admitting the infidelity, whether by independent exposure or reckoning with her own conscience, she would then carefully plan the confession and in explaining the "why," she would usually use the opportunity to cast some type of blame on her partner. In doing so, she usually does not intend to hurt her partner but is hoping that if she could justify her actions, then she could mitigate his response and his post-infidelity opinion of her. In the two scenarios described above, the approach to resolving the infidelity transaction is tainted, as one is preoccupied with protecting while the other is preoccupied with preserving, and a conflict of interests presents itself at the very beginning of any possibility for resolution.

If men and women actually get to the point of being honest as to what caused the infidelity to occur, the woman would begin to list the various problems she has with her man, and the man would itemize the many difficulties he has with the woman. Despite all the justifications that may be offered by either sex as to why the other is unfaithful, infidelity is not simply caused by an unhappy relationship. It is not caused by a man's lack of conversation with or his display of affection to his partner, nor by a woman being a terrible homemaker, nor by her being sexually dissatisfying, or by her being sexually unavailable to her partner. Further, it is not generally or usually caused because persons are evil, uncaring, worthless, or insensitive human beings. Answering this mystery as to why only comes through honesty about one's feelings concerning the relationship and/or one's own independent, internal struggles with being monogamous in the first place.

As mentioned in the previous chapter, persons have come to me for premarital counseling knowing that their partners were simultaneously involved in other relationships. Oftentimes, if the issue is not pressed, the extra relationship is never raised. The issue would surface later in the session, through questioning on the areas of trust and friendship between the two, but it is not a topic the couple wants to discuss during the session.

There are a couple of reasons for this. Until they are married, the level of expectation for faithfulness is much lower for most women. Also, at this point, most women are more concerned about the wedding and less concerned about the nature of the relationship. It is therefore the last thing she wants to discuss for fear of the wedding plans being canceled. The man will not raise the issue either as it is the last thing on earth he wants to discuss anyway.

Both downplay the importance of the discussion in a sort of false hope or unrealistic desire that the marriage will solve the infidelity problem. The man usually deals with this issue from a psychological perspective. He rationalizes that he is making a decision to settle down in a committed space and that eventually (as if by osmosis) all the extra relationships will fall away.

Once the marriage ceremony has taken place however, less tolerance of infidelity is demonstrated by the woman. The woman is often of the view that now that she has been chosen among others, she has won the love, loyalty, and affection of her man and now, given the opportunity to serve him in every way as a wife, that would be enough to keep him committed and from straying. She pledges to commit herself to giving service to her man, particularly in the area of intimacy and sex.

These high standards and goals that are self-imposed by the woman only lead to a greater level of disappointment once post-wedding, the male behavior does not change, no matter how much service—sexual or otherwise—is provided by the female. Depression, anger, and resentment may then set in, all of which serve to undermine the integrity of the marriage and the relationship of the husband and wife.

It also becomes more difficult to answer the question of *why* when the infidelity did not exist or was unknown prior to the marriage. Added to this is the further complication that more seriously affects long-standing marriages where wealth, prosperity, and posterity have been jointly built by the husband and wife. When infidelity is discovered in these types of marriages, because there is so much more at stake, the responses may be more dramatic and the *whys* are typically harder to answer: Why would he put our family at risk? Why would he put the business(es) we built together at risk? Why would he do this to me, to us, to his children? Why … ? Why … ? Why … ?

As a result, many find themselves ultimately despising the person they pledged to love until death separated them, and in extreme circumstances, mental, physical, and emotional abuse or even death can be a resulting consequence. It is one of the reasons that I place great emphasis as a marriage counselor on the charge given during the wedding ceremony: therefore marriage is not to be entered into unadvisedly nor lightly, but soberly and deliberately and in reverenced fear before God.

I can go on, but the point is this: in an effort to really provide some of the answers as to why people are unfaithful, we must first dismiss some of the damaging conclusions that are derived from an emotional place as opposed to one of knowledge, understanding, and proper analysis. People are usually not unfaithful because they are pigs, sows, or he and she dogs as some women and men have suggested. Instead, I offer an alternative explanation.

As humans, having a human sexual drive is a gift given to each person by the Creator. It is therefore innate and does not easily and automatically conform to social regulation. This human sexual drive has been existent in man since the beginning of time (hundreds of thousands of years); whereas, emotional/social monogamy (as reinforced by social norms, rules, and regulation) has only existed for thousands of years. The need for emotional monogamy developed alongside the social focus for strong families, as the family unit is the substratum for strong societies.

On the premise that humans are not monogamous by nature, as the shaping of society continues to evolve, a natural, dominant desire is being forced to contain itself within socially accepted standards, and the dominant desire is prevailing. Hence, when we ultimately choose the complicated, yet attainable goal to commit faithfully to one person without having the appropriate conditions in place (including proper spiritual guidance, no matter the religion), we set ourselves up for hurt, failure, and disappointment.

We must understand and accept our shortcomings and not ignore them. Further, the desire to be monogamous as the wedding vows suggest—forsaking all others so long as you both shall live—and not having the societal construct in place to support the desire and the commitment to be monogamous ultimately culminates in the confused and resigned state of mind most parties to a marriage find themselves in today.

Let me raise an assumption that if provided with better information, knowledge, and platform for discussion, the causes of the infidelity plague can be demystified. Everyone may not agree as to why, but it is hoped that a better understanding of the reasons for the behavior could help to remedy the causes of the fallout. Let me reemphasize then that infidelity is not necessarily the result of unhappiness or the insufficiency of one partner to another. At its root, it is an unbridled human sexuality that over time has increasingly been forced to couple itself with emotional needs and desires.

For a man, this unbridled sexual drive appears to be in more abundance. As a result, the male sex drive is stronger and the desire for sex is more frequent. It seems that the male sex drive has been designed to operate from a raw, physical place, whereas for a woman, it seems to operate from an emotional, affectionate place. A man can therefore have sex with a friend as easily as he can have sex with a stranger. Because of this biological design in the male sexuality, males are also far more stimulated by sight than women. It is also for this reason that an attractive woman would naturally trigger the sexual appetite in males, irrespective of foreknowledge or an underlying relationship.

A woman, on the other hand, will usually need an emotional connection to engage in sex. As a prerequisite, a sense of caring would usually need to be had by her. It is the reason infidelity by women usually occurs within a close-knit circle of family, coworkers, or friends—persons she shares her personal space with and confides in in various ways. It is also the reason many cases of infidelity by women are never discovered. Due to the close nature of the relationships within which the infidelity occurs, the parties are aware of the multiple levels at which these relationships are at stake, and there is more effort to protect those relationships by keeping the infidelity a secret.

Men will visualize, desire, and attempt to conquer, void of any emotional connection or underlying relationship. The desire is based on natural instinct and physical attraction. In these cases, as there are usually no friendships to protect, the probability of the infidelity being exposed by the third party to the infidelity is very high.

Indeed, the human sexual journey is very complicated, and no one answer as to why will create a one-size-fits-all response to all the questions. As we evolve in the next thousands of years, it is yet to be seen whether the emotional need and desire to be monogamous will become the dominant factor that dictates to the human sexual drive. For the moment, the reality is that it is not dominant, and we do see the results of this reality in our lives every day.

As the mystery of monogamy is further explored in the upcoming chapters, while I continue to explore the *why* question of infidelity, I hope to provide some directional tools that can nurture monogamy in interpersonal relationships and help persons to survive committed relationships even when plagued by infidelity. I also hope that the information presented will assist any individual on the receiving end of infidelity to remain emotionally healthy with his or her self-esteem and integrity intact. Hence, it is my belief that the dangers of depression, anger, hatred, and low self-esteem can be minimized by an informed understanding that the battle to achieve fidelity in interpersonal relationships is greater than the individuals themselves.

CHAPTER 6
Why Did I Get Married?

If we are honest, many of us at some stage of our married lives ask ourselves the question: Why did I get married? The rhetorical question is often asked because the marriage is not working out as planned or envisioned, and husbands and wives become anxious and even nauseous about the decision they took to marry in the first place. In the previous chapter, I discussed the difficult goal of committing faithfully and indicated that when we do so without the appropriate conditions in place, the goal is often much harder to realize successfully.

If monogamy is not natural and has not become commonplace by socialization, then what conditions or factors should persons bear in mind when committing to lifetime relationships expecting monogamy? These issues are frequently discussed at length at my church, as we try to focus on the wellness of the whole person and not only the nature of his or her vertical relationship with God. The conditions I explore in this chapter are therefore really a compilation of the many lively discussions we have had on these areas of our Christian walk in Bible study at my church. Thank you, New Life!

Certain conditions that nurture and encourage monogamy should be explored. I have referred to these conditions in this chapter as rules of engagement. Many of these rules are derived from the principles contained in the Holy Bible, because I have found that guidance for everything in my life can be found there. It is a wonder to my world. It stands imposing, as the Rock of Gibraltar, relentlessly resisting the centuries of tsunamis of cultural evolution.

Rule of Engagement #1: Marriage was not designed to make you happy.

Perhaps the most fundamental of the rules of engagement I propose, is that contrary to the expectations of many, marriage is not an institution that was designed to bring instant gratification and happiness. In other words, the marriage institution is not simply pregnant with happiness and joy waiting to shower the parties to it with its goodness. Unfortunately, it does not work as a happy pill. Equally important, marriage will not bring happiness and joy to an otherwise unhappy or sad person. In fact, the reverse is true—an unhappy person would most likely deposit negatively into the marriage instead of withdrawing joyous and happy benefits from it.

Hence, two persons who deal with conflicts of various kinds prior to their marriage, whether they are general conflicts or abuse or infidelity-related conflicts, will, without intervention, experience these same conditions after their marriage. Too often, parties to a marriage go into the situation expecting the marriage to solve all their premarital problems without a full understanding of the purpose for which marriage was designed. A good, successful marriage can be a very happy and gratifying place, but it requires the right conditions, and it takes hard work to keep those conditions fertile and to prevent them from becoming fallow.

To further posit what marriage is not: it is not an institution that can be sustained if built only on passion and romance; it should not be the vehicle that is used to legalize sex; it should not be an institution used for economic alliance due to financial hardship being experienced by one or both parties; and it certainly should not be approached with the mind-set that there is an option of getting out.

If persons embark on marriage with any or all of the above reasons in mind, it only creates an environment for marital disharmony, and the marriage becomes an unhappy place. This then leaves open doors for broken promises; unkept vows; unfulfilled, disrespected, and unappreciated spouses; and loveless marriages; which in turn presents the perfect breeding ground for infidelity.

Rule of Engagement #2: Know the purpose of marriage.
Another critical rule of engagement for couples to understand is the overriding objective of marriage. Marriage was created for our good. The Bible says that he who finds a wife finds what is good and obtains favor from the Lord. Marriage for humans is an earthly version of the heavenly model of the relationship between Christ and His church. As the church is one-half of a serious love relationship for Christ, it is also expected that marriage between a man and a woman would be taken seriously by both. By the point of premarital engagement, in order to fulfill His overriding objective, couples must also understand that marriage was created by God for certain fundamental purposes as follows:

> (a) Firstly, it was designed to provide companionship. Why did God create Eve? She was created because Adam was lonely and he needed a helper and a companion (someone to fellowship with him, help him, and comfort him). She was created to fulfill what was lacking in Adam's life: companionship on his level. In order for companionship and fellowship to blossom, the two parties to the marriage must agree how they will order their lives together and walk together, as the Bible is clear that two cannot walk together except they are agreed. Hence, the woman cannot be firm and uncompromising on monogamy while the man is relaxed and nonchalant on the issue, because a major conflict will arise.

> (b) Marriage was also designed to provide sexual fulfillment and enjoyment without having to resort to acts of sexual immorality to

do so. In its true form, it provides a safe and healthy environment in which we all can express our gift of sexuality without being exposed to the often grave consequences that can result from non-committed sexual relationships.

(c) Another fundamental purpose for marriage is procreation. God also designed marriage for this purpose, and He commanded the first man and woman to be fruitful, to multiply, and to replenish the earth.

(d) Marriage was also created for the protection of all parties to the marriage. Men are called to love their wives as Christ loved the church and laid down His life for it. Hence, a man is expected to protect his wife, even if it means giving his own life in so doing. Men are also called to be temperate, worthy of respect, self-controlled, and sound in faith, love, and endurance. The wife was intended to protect the interests of her children and her home. She is called to love her husband and children, to be self-controlled and pure, to be busy at home, to be kind, and to subject herself to her husband.

Both the husband and wife are jointly called to protect their children and their children's interests. They are required to train up their children in the instruction of the Lord so that when the children are old, they will not depart from it. Marriage was therefore also intended to create a stable environment in which children can be raised to grow and thrive successfully in a godly way.

Just as families are the substratum for strong societies, so is marriage the substratum for strong families. It is the reason that if women in biblical times committed adultery, they were put to death, because to threaten the family is to threaten the peace, safety, stability, and viability of the society. Other religions such as Islam still enforce these laws today for both men and women.

Further, research has shown that the level of dysfunction in any society can be traced to the level of dysfunction in marriage as well as the unbridled sexuality in society. It also shows that when the family breaks down, there is a greater potential for juvenile delinquency, crime, poverty, and lower levels of life achievement.

Marriage was therefore ordained by God for the good of man. Hence, the importance of it and procreating within its confines should be understood by all. As a matter of fact, the Bible states that marriage is honorable among all people. It should be approached as a commitment between the two parties to God, family, and the larger society.

Rule of Engagement #3: Do not fall "in love." Understand it!
Too many people get married because they are "in love," but romantic love alone is almost a guarantee for marital failure. Marriage is a permanent institution and should be built on a permanent foundation of love, which romantic love is not. The Bible speaks about a leaving and a cleaving in marriage. To leave father and mother speaks to a change in the order of priority of a man—from that of his father and mother to that of his wife and family. To cleave speaks of permanence, a commitment for life; therefore, divorce should not be viewed as an option. Is love enough to sustain this permanence?

Western cultures have imported the need for romantic love as a foundational prerequisite for marriage. This is not the approach taken by the Bible however. The commandment in Ephesians 5:25 for husbands to love their wives as Christ loved the church and gave Himself up for her, is not rooted in romantic love. In fact, some of these men (for example, Isaac) in biblical times did not even have the option to be romantically ignited with their wives, because marriages were prearranged with no input from these men at all. Hence, the Ephesians 5 love was not a love based on how the man felt at any given time and was not dependent on how physically attractive his wife was at first sight. The love spoken of in that Scripture is a self-sacrificing, protective, unconditional, and enduring love.

Further, the Bible teaches us that, "love is patient, love is kind. It does not envy, it does not boast, it is not proud. It does not dishonor others, it is not self-seeking, it is not easily angered, it keeps no record of wrongs. Love does not delight in evil but rejoices with the truth. It always protects, always trusts, always hopes, always perseveres. Love never fails" (1 Corinthians 13:4–8 NIV).

This is no ordinary love, and it is on this type of love foundation that marriages should be built. I am always amazed at how much guidance we get from the Bible on how we should order our lives, yet we do not adhere. Each time I read that passage, I wonder how many of us could truly speak that way to describe our love; and it led me to the realization that the struggles we have with our love are perhaps because we do not allow biblical teachings on love to guide us in our decision-making when in pursuit of interpersonal relationships.

It is widely accepted that humans are tri-part beings, possessing a body, soul (will, mind, emotions), and a spirit. Psychologists have also widely recognized three main types of love: eros, philios, and agape. *Eros* is known as romantic, erotic love. It is based on strong feelings toward another and is usually the type of love one sees at the early stages of a man-woman romantic relationship. I reiterate, "You must understand that the touch of your hand makes my pulse react! That it's only the thrill of boy meeting girl, opposites attract. It's physical, only logical. You must try to ignore that it means more than that!" sings Tina Turner. The lyrics of this song could perhaps be the poster song for eros (romantic love). This type of love is based on physical traits (how a person looks, smells, talks, walks; his or her talents and abilities; etc.).

Romantic love has a weak substratum. It is physical (body) at its base; nothing spiritual or mental is involved. At this stage of the relationship, emotions develop almost immediately and are running high, but neither of the parties knows the other well enough to truly say that he or she loves the other. Unless it develops into a stronger form of love, romantic love is usually short-lived and does not last. This type of love is untested by hardship, overcompensates with emotions, and is the reason so many people "fall in love" then out of love with a person they initially thought was an angel sent to them from heaven and nicely packaged by God Himself!

Of course by the time it is recognized that only romantic love was present at the beginning of the relationship, many are settled (whether married or unmarried) with children, pets, mortgages, tuition bills, businesses, car loans, and the list goes on and on. In most cases, the resulting situation can be described as a real predicament.

In contrast to eros, *philios* (friendly love) is a love based on friendship between two people. In this type of love, two people begin by being friends, then comes the admiration (based on the information you learn about the person during the friendship), then the emotions follow over time. As an example, both of you may realize that you miss each other and want to spend time in each other's company even where there is no defined relationship over and above the friendship.

Friendly love has a strong substratum as it is here that our mental element (soul) comes into play. Romantic love still has a place, but it is not the basis of the relationship; it is forced to operate within a setting where there is a type of love from two people who have been friends and are truly fond of and truly admire and appreciate each other. It is really when philios and eros join hands in matrimony that love can be a friendship set on fire!

Agape love is the third and highest form of love. It is selfless and has no need for reciprocation. It is love without benefit, and it is given even if nothing is given in return. It is the type of love the Bible mostly speaks of. The paradigmatic example of this type of love enunciated in the Bible is the verse that says, "Love your enemies, bless them that curse you, do good to them that hate you, and pray for them that despitefully use you and persecute you" (Matthew 5:44 NIV). It is the unconditional love we should all strive for, especially in our interpersonal relationships.

The best human example of agape love is the love a mother or father has for a child and the love a child has for his or her mother or father. It is usually pure love, love no matter what, love against all odds—the 1 Corinthians 13:4 type of love. It is the type of love that born-again Christians believe God has for us and showed to us by way of example, in sending His only Son to die on the cross for our salvation.

This type of love has a spiritual substratum and is rare. However, with humans it can be nurtured and developed over time. Most persons have not given or received love at this high level, and unless we are able to tap into our spiritual being, the majority of us will never be able to experience love at this level during our lifetime.

I am absolutely now convinced that if in interpersonal relationships, love has to suffer long and always be kind, cannot be rude, must resist being easily provoked, refrain from thinking evil, bear all things, hope for good in all things, and endure all things, then friendship (philios) and not romantic love (eros) must be the starting point in order to get to unconditional love (agape).

The overemphasis on romantic love is one of the main reasons married couples do not treat their spouses as they did during the dating period. By the time the challenging event (e.g., infidelity) occurs in the marriage, the initial strong physical attraction is already dead or is on life support. When romantic love dies or is severely weak, most of us come full circle with a person we do not really know and may not even like, whose value system puts us in absolute shock, whose morals and integrity do not align with our own, and whose principles and ideals leave us in utter disbelief.

Nothing is left to support the relationship when friendship or unconditional love was never its foundation. It is the reason I believe that the cause of man's infidelity is deeper than a woman's ability to remain physically attractive over time. That is an eros requirement, and the novelty of the physical attraction of any woman will depreciate with a man over time, no matter how beautiful she is and how well she and her body have aged. The novelty of men will also depreciate over time. In fact, many wives admit that the novelty of their husbands diminishes too, but they complain less about it because they have been socialized to be masters of acceptance!

I should be clear at this stage that romantic love is necessary in marriages, as romance was a part of God's original plan. Romance is natural and very important in strengthening bonds between a man and a woman. It must not, however, be mistaken for friendly or unconditional love, as the other two require a mental and spiritual participation that does not arise from romantic love alone.

When friendly love or unconditional love is foundational to a relationship, the love is at such a high level that even where romance is struggling at times on either side, the unconditional love that has developed or is developing from the friendship places a demand on romantic love to continue to live and find its place in the relationship. Because you love the person completely, the desire for intimacy then comes from a place of acceptance, admiration, appreciation, patience, and all the other variables mentioned in 1 Corinthians 13:4 about love.

Romantic love can therefore only have long life in the atmosphere of friendship or unconditional love. King Solomon understood this very well, and he charged the daughters of Jerusalem, by the gazelles and the does of the field, not to arouse or awaken love until it so desired. In other words, do not excite love, do not stir it up until the time is ripe—and you are ready. He was the wisest man who ever lived!

It is why I am of the view (as suggested in earlier chapters) that the reasons put forward on either side as the causes of infidelity, are more often than not symptoms and not the causes of the infidelity dysfunction in relationships. There are reasons that a wife is disrespectful, unkind, unkempt, unavailable (emotionally and physically), unresponsive, etc., to her husband. She may find that she does not have a friend in her husband, someone who shows himself friendly and who offers friendly love at all times.

There are also reasons a man no longer finds his wife beautiful, attractive, sexy, and appealing. Her physical attractiveness may have been the only feature about her that captured him in the first instance, and if that disappears over time or in no time, then there is nothing left that attracts him to her or to demonstrate her appeal or beauty to him.

The cause of these symptoms must be diagnosed and treated. If it remains undiscovered and untreated, the symptoms will continue to resurface in the relationship, much the same way cancer does in a sick body. Most of us do not want to deal with these hurtful truths about our relationships as we discover the sickness within them. Instead of accepting that the marriage was destined to fail from the outset because of the type of fleeting love it was built on and attempt to attend to these realizations, we resort to keeping up the marriage facade for various reasons and suffer unfulfilment and dissatisfaction in the process.

We must retrain our minds, bodies, and spirits to seek friendship (true intimacy) over quick (fleeting) romance. We must choose partners based on core value systems, principles, ethics, and morals, as opposed to staging beauty and sexual contests. Further, we must teach our children how to choose life partners successfully, as we have now lost many generations of *successful* marriages to the erroneous reliance on romantic love. The Eastern world may be fanatic with the way marriages are prearranged, but I am of the view that the concept of how to choose life partners that underpins socialization in the East more closely mirrors the fundamentals of philios and agape than our socialization in the West, where eros is king.

The truth is that the emotional eros love, when out of place or acting on its own without philios or agape love, is nothing more than a recipe for disaster. The concept of love most of us have been socialized to practice in the West is flawed at its most epistemological level. As a result, it leaves in its wake insecure and disrespectful husbands; miserable and scornful wives; dysfunctional, unhappy, and unproductive children, whom we raise in the *haunted houses* some of us create in our marriages; and marriages that only remain together due to certain financial commitments or dependence that the parties are not able or willing to deal with on their own.

Marriage should therefore be entered into from a knowledge base of the true purposes of marriage, upon friendly terms, and with an unconditional and permanent mind-set. It should definitely not be approached from the emotional place of passion, temporal attraction, romance, or transitional convenience. So, why did *you* get married?

Rule of Engagement #4: Marry your friend.
Rule of engagement #3 leads very nicely into rule #4: Marry your friend! Percy Sledge sings in his 1960s love song, "Take time to know her: it's not an overnight thing." One of the main reasons cited by individuals for marital infidelity and breakups is the notion that

passionate romance followed by good sex is enough to form a lasting bond. On the contrary, where there is sex and romance (as fantastic as they may be) and no friendship, a long-lasting relationship (marital or otherwise) will find itself always dealing with issues such as infidelity.

Friendship—at least in the Western world of love, romance, and marriage—is the key to establishing a long-lasting relationship and to minimizing the likelihood of having an affair. The Bible says that, "a friend loveth at all times" (KJV). It did not say that a husband or a wife loveth at all times. It said a friend. This would suggest that friendship supersedes titles, and it also gives credence to the saying, "a friend in need is a friend indeed." I believe when one finds a friend in his or her lifetime mate, it plays a key role in helping to ensure the permanence and enjoyment of the relationship.

What is a friend? A friend is a person with whom one has a bond of mutual affection. It is a person whom one knows, likes, and trusts. A friend is someone you like to talk to, spend time with, and share secrets; someone who knows your good moods and bad moods; and someone who knows what makes you happy and sad. Such a person is a prime candidate for a permanent relationship, which is the type of relationship that marriage should be.

Rule of Engagement #5: Know that it's the heart that matters most. Persons embarking on a lifetime commitment should ensure that they are inviting persons into their lives that possess a good heart. The Bible also has a lot to say about a good heart. God described David as a man after His own heart. This is in spite of the fact that David's life was considerably flawed. David, as we know, made many mistakes, had several moments of weakness, and as a result, is the reason the story of David and Bathsheba is so well known today. This moment of weakness led to him being an adulterer and subsequently, a murderer when he killed Uriah (Bathsheba's husband) after David had sex with Bathsheba and impregnated her.

David was also violent and brutal at times, and he was later informed that he was forbidden from building God's temple because of some of his actions. Yet he had a heart (i.e. a center, a constitution, a core) that even the ugly truth could not compare with in terms of his legacy. He took responsibility for his wrongs. He became broken and remorseful over his own challenges with his spirituality. As a *Jabez Teen* in my church once said, "His shell got cracked, but his yolk was still good." So, he was always repentant for his wrongs and sought after God like no other had done before or after him.

A good life partner would have a good heart (a David-like heart). As we see from David's life, a good heart does not mean a person who would do no wrong. As a matter of fact, no such person exists! It means that if such a person is involved in wrongdoing, he or she is not stuck perpetually, as the humility of heart would always trigger the desire to correct the behavior and to get back into rightful relationship.

This quality is crucial, and in ordering relationships, men and women should not overly concentrate on the outward appearance but should discover the heart. If the heart is good, then the steps of that man or woman would not continuously or perpetually slip. When he or she does slip, that person is hurt, disappointed, and repentant and will seek forgiveness on all levels. The next logical question may be: How does one detect a good heart? Again, the Bible provides a simple, yet profound answer to this question. A good prospective spouse will produce good things from his or her heart, for out of the overflow of the heart the mouth will speak.

Rule of Engagement #6: Take proper account of the differences in personality types.
Personality types should also be analyzed and taken into account when we are trying to order relationships. Everyone was created for a purpose. Since we were not all created for the same purpose, we were not all designed to operate in the same way. We must therefore

understand how we were designed to operate in this world and also, how the persons who we desire to have relationships with were designed by God. Understanding these personality types is crucial to understanding how to operate with persons who were not designed to operate exactly like us. Psychologists have concluded studies and have grouped behaviors based on several different personality types.

There are many personality traits exercises that can be undertaken. I would personally recommend that every couple takes a Myers-Briggs Personality Type Indicator Test—a personality exercise we recently conducted for the leadership tier at NLBC while in the middle of a restructuring. However, there are many others which can be accessed via the Internet as well, and these can also be utilized in assisting married couples to better understand each other.

Studying these personality types in our relationships helps us to understand when we need to support our partners and assist them once we realize that they are out of control based on their personality types. It helps us to better appreciate that the person is not just evil and heartless, but that he or she needs to be supported back into his or her normal behavior pattern. Understanding personality types therefore fosters patience in relationships and encourages a better support system in a person's spouse/partner, since it is accepted that each person would be affected, at some point or the other, by the vicissitudes of life.

Rule of Engagement #7: Aspire to achieve the God standard for marriage.
The Bible has provided guidance as to how marriage, especially in the Christian household, should look. In Ephesians, men were admonished to love their wives as Christ loved the church and gave Himself up for her. The love described therein is a love that goes the distance and is marked by giving and not receiving.

Wives were also admonished to submit themselves unto their own husbands, for the husband is the head of the wife as Christ is the head of the church. As the church submits to Christ, so also wives should submit to their husbands in everything. Now women usually try to pretend that this Scripture doesn't exist because it is viewed negatively, especially by modern-day women. When they do so, however, they act to their detriment and will more often than not, face marital dilemma.

Submission, in the biblical context, does not mean yielding to a higher authority out of weakness. Rather, it means to possess a voluntary attitude of giving in, cooperating, and sharing a burden—in the order God decided in His infinite wisdom for the household to operate within. The Bible also guides us in Ephesians 5, where it says that each (both man and woman) is to submit to the other out of reverence to Christ. The Bible is also instructive as to how the husband should handle his God-given authority. Peter cautions,

> In the same way, you husbands must give honor to your wives. Treat your wife with understanding as you live together. She may be weaker than you are, but she is your equal partner in God's gift of new life. Treat her as you should so your prayers will not be hindered. (1 Peter 3:7)

The responsibility toward the marriage is therefore on both parties, and each one has a role, which neither is to abuse.

Men, the Proverbs 31 woman should not be ignored when you are making the important life decision of choosing a wife. The Bible has a lot to say about how this type of woman operates, and the model has become the ideal standard. Although the standard is not easily achievable, it is much desired. Much of the text of Proverbs 31 may seem old-fashioned today, but some relevant and substantive principles can still be extracted. They are as follows:

- She is trustworthy. Because of this, her husband has everything he needs, and she will greatly enrich his life. She provides a safe haven for her husband. She loves him, and he has confidence in her integrity and good character.

- She is industrious (whether as a housewife or a career wife or a mixture of both). She is not lazy and makes sure that her household is properly taken care of. She is reliable.

- She is wise in investments. She does not waste money.

- She works as long and hard as she has to in order to ensure that her enterprises are profitable. She is always busy and productive.

- She is generous and is always ready to help others. She does not worry about challenging (winter) seasons in her life, because she has prepared her household to deal with challenges.

- She can help herself and does not need to rely on others to do everything for her. She dresses in the finest of garments.

- She has a husband who is well-respected and who is concerned about national affairs.

- She does not worry about her future, so she is always happy. She speaks words of wisdom, and when she gives advice, she does so from the heart. She concerns herself and keeps a close eye on everyone and everything in her household and does not allow laziness to cloud her vigilance.

- She teaches her children the ways of the Lord and trains them in the way they should go. Her children respect her, and she is praised by her husband. She is the cream of the crop to her family.

- She understands that charm is deceptive and beauty has its time. Therefore, her spiritual being is most important to her, so she fears the Lord.

- Because of who she is, she will be rewarded and her deeds will speak publicly for her.

Those are the qualities of a wife of noble character.

Women, in examining the way the Proverbs 31 woman operates, a man of similar character to the Proverbs 31 man should also exist. It would be good to pay attention to the positive characteristics of this man when deciding upon a husband, leader, protector, and father of your children:

- He should not be controlling or manipulative. He should be trusting of his wife.

- He should not be selfish. His wife could not be charitable if he did not agree or there would be friction in the household.

- He should procreate only within a marriage with his wife. He should not birth children out of wedlock.

- He would be involved with business and enterprise and accesses the presence of important people. Since he can trust his wife with his personal and family affairs, he is free to concern himself with national matters that affect the city where he lives.

- He is not violent or wasteful. He is stable and committed, and he loves and desires God.

- He knows and understands the importance of praising his wife.

- He too must realize the inner beauty of his wife and understands that physical beauty is temporal. He is not overly impressed with physical beauty and charm. He is a man who would be more impressed with kindness, loyalty, integrity, a noble character, and a woman who fears the Lord.

The Proverbs 31 standard is set very high and because of this, it is very discouraging to most; yet it is a standard that every dating, engaged, and married couple should aspire to. Each individual desiring a successful marriage should make a serious attempt at modeling the behavior of the parties within the Proverbs 31 household, even while dating or before dating. Practice makes perfect! Just as we continue to work toward perfection in our Christianity, God expects us to do no less with our marriages.

In addition to the above rules, Christian couples should also pay as much attention to Ephesians 5:18–21 as they do to verses 22–33 of that chapter (the specific instructions for husbands and wives). Verses 18 to 21 admonish Christian couples to: (1) avoid becoming drunk as drunkenness dissipates anything; (2) be filled with the Spirit; (3) encourage each other by singing psalms, hymns, songs of worship, and praise; (4) always be in a praiseful and prayerful posture; (5) live and exist in a constant state of gratefulness and gratitude to God; and (6) submit willingly to one another, if for no other reason, out of reverence and fear of Christ.

Finally, couples should also bear in mind that pitfalls will always need to be avoided, challenges will still present, and problems are likely to manifest. A marriage is as much a living, breathing institution as the organisms who are parties to it, and as long as it is living, it will continuously evolve, adapt, and mutate. However, if we engage these rules, take them seriously, and apply them to our lives prior to and during marriage, they would go a long way in providing an environment in which monogamy can thrive and the question, "Why did I get married?", could be answered informatively, intelligently, positively, and with a smile.

CHAPTER 7
Can You Handle the Truth?

There is no doubt that the majority of people in society—married or unmarried—have a strong desire to be faithful in our relationships. It is not only an expectation but a serious desire to be faithful. It is reflected in our wedding vows, and when we agree to forsake all others and be faithful to each other so long as we both shall live, it is an agreement most of us take seriously. There seems to be a level of disconnect however, between the desire to be faithful and the natural proclivity that drives the behavior that leads to unfaithfulness. Hence, the evidence will show that the mind-set to be faithful is there, but the issue of how to accomplish it proves, for most, to be challenging at best.

For the purpose of this book, a survey was designed, and 150 men and women were surveyed around the issue of infidelity. It is important to note that the majority of those surveyed were members of the Christian community. On the issue regarding the importance of being faithful (monogamous) in a relationship, more than 90 percent of those men and women surveyed over the age of twenty-one felt that it was extremely important to them to be faithful in their relationships. Reasons cited for the importance of being faithful included stability, health (prevention of the spread of sexually transmitted diseases), building strong families, and creating true intimacy and trust in relationships.

However, when asked whether it was natural for a man to have more than one female sexual partner at a given time, 59 percent of men said yes, and 46 percent of the women agreed with them. When this same question was reversed (i.e., whether it was natural for a woman to have more than one male sexual partner at a given time), only 27 percent of men and 21 percent of women agreed that it was natural.

It is apparent that on both questions, both the men and women agree that it is more natural for a man to have more than one female sexual partner. The survey results also supports the view put forward earlier in this book that there is an obvious double standard in the thought processes as to the expectation for faithfulness by men and women in their relationships which does not play out in practice.

When the question was posed: Have you ever been unfaithful in a marriage or committed relationship?—i.e., following through on a desire to having more than one sexual partner—one-third of the women surveyed said yes, and twice as many men as women admitted to following through on this desire and had therefore been unfaithful. Fifty-eight percent of married men and women admitted to being faithful in their marriages; the other forty-two percent having admitted to being unfaithful.

This result should really come as no surprise. On the bright side, it offers hope that when two persons commit themselves to the ideal of monogamy and allow the tenets of monogamy to order the value systems governing their interpersonal relationships, it can be achieved—and from the survey results, *is* being achieved in a fair amount of cases. It is also instructive to note that persons responding in the forty-one–to–fifty-five age category had the highest incidences of infidelity with nearly 50 percent of them being married women. This result gives credence to the view put forward in earlier chapters that women cheat as much or nearly as much as men, although the societal perception runs contrary to this idea.

Another question posed in the survey, was whether persons who had never had an affair would have an affair if they were absolutely certain that they would not be caught. Interestingly, only 5 percent of women admitted that they would cheat if they knew for sure they would not be caught, and only 18 percent of men said they would.

However, when the same question was asked more generally, whether they thought people would cheat if they knew they would not be caught – 77 percent of men and 70 percent of women said yes; 55 percent of the women who said yes were married or in a committed relationship and all of the men who were married or in a committed relationship agreed with them. Generally, 69 percent of the married people surveyed indicated that they thought that people would cheat if they knew they would not be caught, and 62 percent of persons not married but in a committed relationship indicated that they thought people would also cheat in these circumstances. These results demonstrate that although the majority of persons surveyed did not admit to being individually challenged with infidelity, there is an obvious recognition and acknowledgement that the challenge to remain monogamous does exist in the wider society; the results further demonstrate that this challenge magnifies in circumstances where persons are convinced that there are no consequences for their behavior.

Although a relatively small sample size, the responses to the questions and the relative percentages are consistent with the globally reported statistics taken from larger samples of populations, and confirm the view that the natural tendency of the majority of both men and women, married or unmarried, if not bridled by spiritual conviction, the fears of societal shame, or relational disruption or destruction, is not to be monogamous.

Another important question posed in the survey was whether a person's partner/spouse had ever been unfaithful to him or her. In responding, 55 percent of married women admitted to their spouse being unfaithful, while 84 percent of unmarried women admitted to having had partners that cheated. Additionally, 60 percent of unmarried but committed women admitted to having been cheated on. Thirty-three percent of the men surveyed indicated that they had been cheated on by their spouse or partner while 67 percent indicated that they had not been cheated on. In general, 83 percent of persons who were unmarried admitted to having been cheated on compared to 47 percent of married persons. These results have therefore further strengthened the position put forward herein that monogamy is not natural, since anything natural would be achieved much more easily and would be the norm and not the exception.

These are the hard truths that we all must face, and the results of this survey emphasize the mystery surrounding monogamy. It is an optimistic expectation of those who commit themselves to lifetime relationships or marriages to believe that the promises and vows they make would somehow immunize them from being unfaithful or experiencing unfaithfulness. The sad truth is that it is not so. The happy truth, however, is that there is hope.

Happily ever after is obviously for fairy tales, but finding meaningful, joyous living in the context of relationships and marriage should be the desire of all. It can be found by those who equip themselves with the knowledge and the understanding of monogamy and commit themselves to this God idea in helping them to achieve one of the greatest desires of the human race: a successful monogamous relationship, the highest level of all human relationships.

CHAPTER 8
Keeping the Wrongdoer; Forgiving the Wrong

Infidelity is destructive, and the effects of infidelity, whether in the context of marriage or in an otherwise committed relationship, are felt at every level—from the impact it has on the individuals involved, including any children, to the impact it has on the societal level. There is no minimizing or sugarcoating of the emotional distress or pain felt by the affected persons. Emotional responses are usually derived from a place of hurt, disappointment, and anger. They leave little or no room for discussion around the root cause or reason for the infidelity and are a hindrance to a survival path for the relationship.

Even where the relationship itself survives the effects of infidelity, unless it undergoes a full and proper recovery, it is often void of trust, true intimacy, and a sustainable comfort level. In such situations, love and respect are lost in the emotional upheaval, and the result is usually an empty shell of a marriage or relationship. This creates a vicious cycle as either or both parties then find themselves in a relationship that is unfulfilling, and they may consequently seek fulfillment outside of the relationship.

It is my belief however, that many good relationships are lost in the fog of misunderstanding and emotions and abruptly come to an end, leaving two people, who have shared so much for so long, as enemies and strangers. Persons who were once loved have crossed over the thin line and are now hated. As a result of these emotional reactions, children are often forced to grow up without having both their mother and father (who in many cases, are jointly good parents to them) in the same household. I am of the view that this ought not be and that interpersonal relationships, whether within a marriage or otherwise, can survive infidelity when provided with the proper counsel and information about infidelity (inclusive of the causes), and where there is a willingness of both parties to maintain the relationship and seek the necessary support to do so.

One of the considerations in surviving infidelity is whether a partner who has cheated or been unfaithful is no longer worthy of the other partner's affection, respect, and trust, no matter what other good qualities the wrongdoer may have. The proverbial question then becomes whether in the event of an infidelity, a person should throw out the baby with the bathwater.

Having considered the issue, I believe that if I had an otherwise good wife and for some reason or the other, she became entangled in an extramarital affair and an infidelity occurred, I would not immediately form the view that the particular situation disqualifies her from my love. The infidelity would not, in my view, automatically mean the end of the marriage.

Of course, I would be hurt, my affection toward her might be suspended, and I would feel disrespected. I may temporarily lose some semblance of respect for her, and my trust in her may diminish, but all those variables could be built back up just as they were broken down. I believe then that we should always consider the character of the person we are in relationship with, separate and apart from the incidence of infidelity, before we make hasty and life-changing decisions on the basis of it.

The Monogamy Mystery

Why should couples try to work out their differences even where there is infidelity? For starters, the wedding vows made between spouses that were taken before God and family at the establishment of the union should really mean something. In those vows, most of us promised to love, to cherish, and to honor. We promised to do so in all situations, whether rich or poor, whether in sickness or in health, and whether for better or for worse.

Infidelity is an example of the *worse*, and while we did promise to love, cherish, and honor through it, most of us find ourselves unwilling or unable to do so if it does present itself in our marriage. Importantly here, while in Matthew 5:32 and Matthew 19:9, sexual immorality or fornication (which is *porneia* in Greek) is provided as an exception to remaining within a marriage, this Scripture is only permissive and not obligatory.

God Himself also provides authority on this available compromise in Hosea, when He commanded Hosea to reconcile with his adulteress wife. Hosea even paid fifteen shekels of silver for his wife to return to him from the man she had been committing adultery with. In doing so, God demonstrated to Hosea and the children of Israel that He still loved them and desired relationship with them, even though they too were committing spiritual adultery by following other gods. Hence, if divorce was obligatory in the instance of adultery, God would not have gone back on His Word in commanding Hosea to reunite with his adulterous wife.

In Malachi 2:16, the Lord is clear that He hates divorce. In Matthew 19:8, He also clarifies that Moses permitted divorce only because of the hardness of men's hearts, but that it was not so from the beginning. Why should couples strive to survive infidelity? Because, where a marriage has any chance of surviving its lethal effects, couples should certainly make a valiant attempt to avoid divorce, whenever possible, as it was never intended in the beginning that marriages should end in divorce, even when infidelity provides the exit clause.

In addition to being mindful of God's permanent idea for marriage, couples should also bear in mind the economic and psychological consequences that usually arise from a divorce. In this context, as sexist as it sounds, the phrase, "It's cheaper to keep her," has logic. Divorce is a growing problem, and it is unapologetically harsh on families.

Based on statistics from the US Census Bureau, divorce has steadily increased over the years from 14 percent in 1920 to just over 50 percent today! It divides assets that could otherwise be multiplied. It can turn two people who procreated beautifully together into bitter enemies where the focus becomes the fight between them and not the best interests of their children. It separates children from being raised in a household with both their parents. It destroys the stability of children and aborts any ability for children to be able to take forward their childhood experience as a good example from which to model their own family structure.

Children become resentful, bitter, hurt, and lost; they lose self-esteem, seek love elsewhere, perform poorly in school, drop out of school, and turn to drugs and/or promiscuity; and unless the children are emotionally strong or stable enough, a divorce can have effects upon them that are detrimentally life lasting. I have also seen adults lose their self-esteem and their self-confidence. They become depressed, some lose their jobs, others have nervous breakdowns, and the list can go on ad infinitum.

In many cases, where the marriage or relationship broke down irretrievably, there is also great resistance by one or both parties in trusting another person enough to embark on or successfully maintain another relationship. Infidelity however, does not need to result in the breakdown of a relationship and produce the grave consequences listed above. Like any other problem, it has a root that has caused the relationship to be unfruitful. If we can find the root and treat it, the relationship can become vibrant again. We can resume enjoying the fruits of the renewed relationship, and we can stabilize our families and keep them together.

I now turn to some helpful solutions and instructions for surviving infidelity, whether it is on a personal level (i.e., self-esteem, confidence, or stability of emotions), a relationship level (keeping the good man or woman while forgiving his or her bad behavior), or truly restoring the marital bond (rediscovering love, restoring respect, encouraging affection, rebuilding trust, and reviving friendship). From my years of experience in this painful area of life, I have concluded that there are five main ingredients that are required if a relationship is to survive infidelity successfully.

Honesty

Firstly, the person committing the affair has to be honest about whether he or she wants the affair to end and his or her marriage to survive. He or she also has to be honest about what is the cause of the unfaithful behavior. I have found that when honesty about one's weaknesses or problem is met with truth and information, it can be the beginning of restoration of lost love and commitment in a relationship.

As an example, I have found over the course of my life journey as a Christian, that the Devil does not tempt me with power or pride. He does not tempt me with loving money and materialism. He does not tempt me with stealing, cursing, alcoholism, or drugs. He has not been able to pose challenges to me loving my enemies, blessing those who curse me, doing good to those who hate me, praying for those who despitefully use and persecute me, nor forgiving those who have wronged me. These have been the greatest challenge to others but not for me. The greatest temptation I have had to overcome was being attracted to and desiring other women outside of my primary interpersonal relationship. It took me a while, but I had to come to the honest realization that this was indeed my challenge.

As a successful businessman, senior pastor of the New Life Baptist Church, a bishop, a public figure with significant political influence, and with a high level of popularity and affluence throughout the British Virgin Islands and the Caribbean, for many years, I enjoyed significant financial and public success but had a private struggle.

The struggle was private because, contrary to anything that we may have seen in most biblical male characters except for Jesus, in the eyes of the church, a pastor is placed on a pedestal as one who should be void of the weaknesses, sexual and otherwise, that may be common to man. Hence, a pastor is often dehumanized by the church. He is expected to walk blameless based on the higher level of relationship he has with God through the spiritual office he holds.

It is important to note however, that the call of God on one's life into ministry is not qualified by some moral standard. Even during their teenage years when persons have not yet spiritually matured or begun to understand life from a natural or spiritual standpoint, the call of God is on their lives, and this immaturity coupled with a spiritual calling presents a greater human challenge. Moreover, although the church will recite the pertinent Scripture over and over again, when it comes to infidelity, the expectation from the church has no real regard for the consideration of the Scripture that the call and gifting of God is without repentance.

It follows that to admit to a struggle, contrary to this high standard of expectation, whether it is sexual desire, alcoholism, drugs, pornography, or otherwise, is to destroy the faith and trust in, and the perception of the leader held by the members of the church. Further, within my interpersonal relationships, I have realized that women are always willing and able to accept any other struggle that may present itself in a relationship by the man except for a struggle by the man that includes a desire for other women. Women may carry on in the relationship, but they never understand this particular struggle.

From the public's eye too, while the pastor is not necessarily put on a pedestal, it is not expected that a man of the cloth would have the same challenges as a non-Christian man would have. So, besides God, who do you tell? Who can you share this struggle with when it seems that no one understands? Who is there to provide the help and support? Further, most pastors, although they can identify with the same types of struggles, would attempt to deal with their struggle privately while they preach to the contrary, publicly. Consequently, most pastors and church leaders suffer from silent confession with no one to trust and no human help availing itself.

In light of all that has been said, I should say at this point that my explanation is not intended to be a justification for my actions or the actions of any other pastor or person in a similar situation for that matter, but it is intended to bring clarification as to why people struggle privately with infidelity, are never able to honestly own it and get the necessary help, and as a result never transform.

In order for me to have even begun to try to overcome this proclivity, the first step I had to take was to own it as my weakness. In order to rectify the problem, I had to stop blaming my interpersonal circumstances and my socialization and admit that I had a problem. I had to muster up the courage to be honest, the willingness to admit to my weakness, and the faith in the people I lead and loved to understand my weakness and support me through the struggle.

At a marriage retreat our church once hosted, I recall the facilitator giving his personal testimony as to how his marriage was able to survive his own unfaithfulness. He explained that he had an affair and that he had admitted and apologized for his indiscretion to his wife. At the time of the admission, they were married for thirteen years and had three children together. The wife, upon hearing the confession, was hurt, shocked, and in tears for some period of time. In the aftermath of the confession, he held his wife and comforted her during her period of suffering, and importantly, she allowed him to do this even though he was the sole cause of her need to be held and comforted.

He informed the persons in attendance at the retreat that after some time had passed and his wife had dealt with the initial shock of the confession, she called him to come to her, asked him to place his head in her lap, and at that point reassured him of her love for him. She thanked him for his honesty and promised to be his greatest support in his efforts to overcome any temptations to be drawn into similar situations with other women.

He then gave her permission to alert him and bring to his attention any signs that she thought might become a problem for him and the marriage, and which could lead to unfaithfulness. His wife in turn gave him the liberty to always be honest with her about his feelings and any matter affecting their relationship, no matter how much he thought it would hurt her. It was one of the most powerful reconciliation stories I had ever heard on infidelity occurring in a Christian home.

It is in this type of environment of ownership, honesty, and transparency, and a willingness to listen, support, and help as a true partner that relationships can survive the destructive nature of infidelity. By the time he gave the testimony, the marriage had grown stronger; they were then married for twenty-five years and had added three more children to the family. They had taken a new approach to the marriage and it was transformed, not simply restored to its previous position. But it was a better marriage than it ever was before.

Friendship

A second ingredient in surviving infidelity and a core environment required for encouraging honesty and transparency is the need for friendship. At the heart of any lasting and viable relationship, there is friendship. A friendship should have the following four core variables: *acceptance*, *respect*, *love*, and *trust*. A relationship that is built on these core living values provides an atmosphere for one to be honest and transparent.

When friendship with others allows you to accept those persons as they are, respect them in spite of who they are, trust who they are, and love them because of who they are, it creates a level of comfort in those relationships that affords a person the privilege of being honest. As difficult as infidelity is to discuss and confess, when those four elements of friendship exist, they create a foundation of confidence, comfort, and security in the relationship where honesty is encouraged.

Hence, honesty is not secured in a vacuum. There must be supporting elements in order to encourage a person to be honest. Generally, a person would shun being honest if he or she knows that punishment, condemnation, or ostracizing would follow. When one knows that there is a friendship with the particular person who knows and accepts him or her, then it is easier to risk the consequences of being honest about a particular situation. In a friendship, such a person would take ownership of the wrong by being honest, and there would be openness and transparency with their partners about the situation.

There is nothing more liberating than the ability to be honest about who you are as a person, being yourself, and feeling comfortable in expressing yourself whether or not the subject matter is as ugly and uncomfortable as infidelity.

A Repentant Heart

Along with honesty and friendship, there is need for a repentant heart if infidelity is to be overcome. We discussed the need to have a repentant heart in relationships in chapter 6. In order for the relationship to be rebuilt, there must be some evidence that both parties still love each other and want to be in relationship with each other. It therefore requires the party committing the wrong to be genuinely repentant about the wrong. He or she must be sorry for the actions and the consequences caused by the actions. Importantly, the wronged party must believe that the heart of the party who wronged him or her is repentant. Therefore, communication of the repentance to the wronged party is required.

A friend of mine once witnessed a situation in a marriage where a man (who had become accustomed to having indiscretions) had a much scandalized affair. When his wife found out about it, he did not admit and apologize to his wife. Instead, he provided an eventual nonchalant, disrespectful and uncaring admission of the indiscretion to his wife (after realizing— following weeks of denial that he could no longer deny the infidelity).

Although the wife eventually forgave him, she thought that the response was so unrepentant that it did nothing to convince her that he cared about the relationship, loved her, or had any care or concern for her feelings at all. An unrepentant heart will not lead to a successful and sustained attempt at surviving infidelity. In the situation immediately above, the marriage was not reconciled and ended in divorce.

Forgiveness

As hard as it is, we are called to forgive. Jesus said in Matthew 6:14–15 (KJV), "For if you forgive men when they sin against you, your heavenly Father will also forgive you. But if you do not forgive men their sins, your Father will not forgive your sins." Infidelity, like all sins, is therefore forgivable. Once the decision is made to survive the infidelity, forgiveness is also a key element in surviving it.

Forgiveness, in its true sense, in the context of surviving infidelity, means to let go of a wrong and not allow any residue of that wrong to remain as a hindrance to the relationship. Just as Christ forgives us as sinners, we must be able to forgive the wrong occasioned on us by another, with a view to be reconciled with that person, trust that person again, be intimate again with that person, and restore joy to the relationship.

It is also important that we do not allow ourselves to be a hindrance to the relationship by not forgiving ourselves for the wrongdoing. God forgives our sins. In 1 John 1:9 (NIV), He says, "If we confess our sins, he is faithful and just and will forgive us our sins and purify us from all unrighteousness." We should therefore also let go of our past actions and not let them consume us into believing that we are not worthy of forgiveness, as this too would hamper any sustainable efforts in reconciling our relationships.

Emotional Support

Emotional support to each other is also critical in surviving infidelity. In this regard, it is also very helpful to take a stroll down memory lane to revisit the days when the relationship was at the place where it was enjoyable by both. The attention, attraction, affection, and the satisfaction of the basic needs of each other that sustained it then, plays a very important role in helping it to survive when it hits a snag.

With a woman in particular, one of her greatest needs in helping her to overcome the pain and disappointment of the affair is the need for emotional support. She needs to be reassured that she is loved; she needs to be held; and she needs attention and affection. Men need to recognize then, that women are more emotional creatures than they are and that this type of emotional support is paramount in helping her to cope with and survive infidelity.

At the same time, women need to understand that during this time of recovery, the man also has needs. His greatest need during this recovery period is for the woman to maintain her respect for him and understand him. His greatest desire is for the woman to understand and believe him that whatever the cause of the infidelity, it was not his intention to hurt her or make her feel inadequate.

Men then are more logical creatures and respond better to responses not solely dictated by emotions; and as difficult as the situation may be, women ought to bear this in mind as well. In addition to the above, godly counsel will also prove to be a very beneficial tool to persons who desire to restore the relationship and are willing to take the necessary steps as summarized above.

In circumstances where the man is the victim of the infidelity, women also need to be sensitive to man's needs. Most men in this situation may need space, more silence than usual and reassurance of his manhood. Women may find that they experience angry outbursts from men in these circumstances. The most helpful position for women in this situation is to be as receptive, available and understanding as she possibly can.

Meet Sarah, a member of my church. Sarah is a born-again believer. When I interviewed her to share a part of her marriage experience for this chapter, she reiterated to me that she firmly believes that in the beginning God created man; and then He took from the rib of man and created a woman. Together they became the first couple, Adam and Eve.

She further confirmed to me that she always held the firm view that marriage between a man and a woman was ordained by God and therefore as the Bible teaches, a man should leave father and mother—*and*, she added, all other women—and cleave to his wife, the woman he vowed to love and to cherish for the rest of their lives. She explained that with those beliefs firmly held,

> It was therefore an earth-shattering, mind-boggling, devastating feeling to suddenly have the rude awakening that the love of my life, the one I have shared more years together as a couple than we both have each lived apart, both of us being brought together by fate on that wonderful, unforgettable day; that this totally devoted, committed person I had put all my love and trust in had just done the unthinkable! He had become engaged in an extramarital affair.
>
> I cannot adequately describe the overwhelming feeling of betrayal I experienced when I learned that the man I loved had been having a secret obsession with another woman. Immediately my mind raced back in time to the day we exchanged our sacred vows, then fast-forwarded to the present situation I faced, with my heart beating so fast, my chest was visibly moving with each thump at the thought that our vows had been violated by my spouse; and yet, at the same time, I felt the need to be protective. Yes, protective of my relationship as strange as that may seem and also protective of my family, more specifically, our children. In my mind they could not be exposed to this revelation about their dad. I still wanted to protect his image in their eyes and I also wanted to protect him from everybody else.
>
> I needed to know the truth; but of course there was denial to begin with and then came the half-truths; but after insisting, not with anger or aggression but in a strange way with love and a kind of empathy, the confession came. It was met with tears of relief and release from both of us and almost immediately, the healing process began. However, it took at least twelve months for the mental fatigue brought on by this experience to subside and for me to feel

almost normal in my sexual relationship with my spouse again, although I went through the motions.

Of course for him, once the confession was made, within a month or so life was as usual, as if nothing had happened. We have to give credit to our men, they have an amazing ability to compartmentalize and move on, but it is not so for us women; our emotions are front and center in all of this, so it takes time for us to come to terms with such devastations in our lives.

Nevertheless, after all I went through in this situation, I was able to forgive the sin of my spouse and keep our marriage alive and well by loving him through his fault even though the memories lingered on in my mind for months and while his memories were seemingly short-lived. I was able to forgive the sin and keep the sinner—my husband—because I willed myself to refrain from rehashing or reminding him of what he had done. Instead I focused on the wonderful relationship we had built together, the beautiful family we created, and the fact that I knew he loved me and that I loved him. I asked God to help me to overcome the emotional pain that the betrayal had caused me; recognizing that like my spouse, I too am just a sinner saved by grace. In doing so we were able to rebuild our relationship over time on love, trust, and commitment, the foundation upon which we first started our lives together.

My advice to those parties to a marriage who have experienced infidelity in their relationships is this: If you are serious about saving your marriage, then stop rehashing or reminding your spouse of what he or she did five years ago or even a year ago. If he or she has moved on with his or her life (putting the infidelity behind), then you should move on with your spouse and work on rebuilding your relationship with God as the third person in your triangle.

Since the infidelity, we have shared many happy years of marriage. Today, we have a solid marriage of over thirty-five years that has been tested. We share our life and love together; we have raised our children together; and now we get to experience our grandchildren together. Forgiveness is worth it and both of you can make it, with God's help.

Sarah has shared another real testimony on the power of forgiveness over infidelity in marriage, and I thank her for doing so. I pray that her testimony blesses you and is helpful to anyone facing those circumstances. We can conclude this chapter in recognition from all of the forgoing, that marital infidelity is destructive to marriages, as marriages were designed to involve a level of intimacy not possible in any other human relationship. It was intended to join two people together as one flesh. The parties to a marriage become vulnerable, expect to be protected by the commitment made to each other, and will lay down their guards regarding their bodies, soul, and heart in this type of environment without fear.

Due to the high level of trust that is expected in a marriage, discovery of infidelity is undoubtedly a devastating blow; but with God's help, recovery is possible through honesty, friendship, a repentant heart, forgiveness, and the proper emotional support. And importantly, such recovery can lead to a stronger and better marriage.

CHAPTER 9
God Help Us All: Spirituality

Spirituality is the personal transformation of a person in accordance with religious beliefs. The many factors that form part of our spiritual indoctrination include theology (our religious beliefs and understanding of the nature of God), love, trust, hope, life circumstances, disillusionment, anger, fear, and death. For many people, the sociological factors will marry the spiritual factors in their pursuit to being accepted in the society in which they live; but for others who are not spiritual, the sociological factors would play the dominant role in informing their thought processes as to how to be accepted by society.

Persons who live from a more spiritual place, and in particular Christians, justify their behavior on their spiritual beliefs and biblical teachings more so than, for example, the socioeconomics of socialization. It is therefore the theology of Christians that should govern how they behave. Theology can inform expectations, shape understanding of right and wrong, and emphasize and reemphasize morals and ethical standards.

Christians would therefore strive for love, trust, and hope within their interpersonal relationships, yet the battle between biology and theology still finds its place. Expectedly or unexpectedly, Christians also find themselves in a state of disillusionment, and experiencing anger and fear in interpersonal relationships. If we are to have any chance of longevity and success in our relationship life, even as Christians, it is important to understand why human beings behave the way we do.

Theology is important in both Western and Eastern societies. Eastern theology would appear to support the acceptance of polygamous behavior in most societies, while Western theology would appear to support monogamous behavior. As more scientific evidence continues to come to light, the theology of Christians will need to continuously justify that the premise that the divine morality that governs the life of Christians is eternal, unchanging, and lasting throughout all time and circumstances.

If the facts are correct and the evidence bears out that monogamy is not a natural function of the biological makeup of human beings, then the following questions can be raised:

- Is there a spiritual response to these issues that scientists are raising— challenging monogamy as a legitimate expectation?
- Can an omniscient, loving, merciful God sentence a person to hell for an action that he or she has no control over?
- Can we or should we continue to ignore the state of our societies and the evidence that indicates that the human animal struggles with monogamy?
- Can we really conclude that the question as to whether human beings can be monogamous is simply one of individual effort, so that where a person fails to be monogamous, he or she is simply not trying hard enough or is just willful?
- Do we accept that there are biological factors at play that constantly compete with our will to do what is acceptable?
- Is the expectation to be monogamous a realistic and achievable expectation for those in committed relationships?
- Is the issue indeed an everlasting war of the flesh and the spirit that Christian humans can only win if they bring the flesh in subjection to the spirit?

- Can the flesh truly be made subject to the spirit?

These are all pregnant questions that should be examined carefully, as the answers to some of them may actually challenge the beliefs and the theology of Christians. Christians in particular, condemn infidelity and believe that faithfulness in a marriage is required by God. Adultery and fornication are therefore sins that Christians believe the Bible cautions against and that are punishable by God.

If the ability to form strong bonding with one's partner and resist infidelity depends on particular hormones and genes, then one may argue as to whether it is fair for a person to be punished for what Christians deem a sin (which in extreme cases, is punishable eternally by the person being cast into hell) for what may really be a genetic problem. The corollary is that the psychology of Western societies has caused these societies to be ordered so that the societal systems support those who are monogamous.

Blame and rejection is therefore cast in the way of those who cannot remain monogamous, and in most societies, these persons are frowned upon (especially when they hold certain positions that are deemed to be esteemed in society) and are castigated as rebels, immoral beings, and in severe cases, social outcasts. This labeling however, solves nothing, and the struggle with monogamy and the consequences of infidelity continue to plague the society.

In the movie, *Hyde Park on the Hudson*, the plot portrayed the story of various love affairs between President Franklin D. Roosevelt and different women including his secretary, but primarily with his distant cousin, Margaret "Daisy" Suckley. At the end of the movie, Daisy said, "In a world where there were still secrets, Franklin was mine."

FDR was not alone in this struggle. Information revealed about various national leaders in America, past and present, would demonstrate that while FDR had his Daisy; JFK also had his Marilyn; and

Clinton, his Monica. Information revealed by Abernathy in his 1989 autobiography indicated that Martin Luther King Jr. had numerous extramarital affairs, and the struggle with women was pointed out as his greatest weakness.

Whether it is president, preacher, priest, or just your regular Joe, I know of very few men who do not struggle with this issue. The question is: If it is a struggle, what then are we struggling against? What is it that society and religion expect of us—that good, decent, and otherwise moral humans find so difficult to achieve? I submit that we are fighting against our very nature, and it is a fight we won't win on our own.

Monogamy then, while an admirable and highly esteemed social ideal, is not achievable by civil or social laws, wedding vows, or religious creed no matter how well attempted the socialization process is. It is a mistake therefore to continue to ignore the fact that monogamy is a serious and real human struggle.

It is not a natural human trait to be monogamous, and it is also a mistake to believe that being monogamous is simply a matter of natural effort and practice without more. Our biological makeup cannot simply be ignored, because history has recorded that monogamy is uncommon to man, no matter their color, race, culture, or creed. Every day there are men or women cheating on each other, or husbands or wives being unfaithful to each other. It is present and evident in our society, and that the problem exists is not one of speculation or debate; it is a fact of life. Polygamous behavior is a norm and is legal in many cultures and societies.

In societies where polygamy (formal marriage between a man and more than one woman in this context) is not legal, polygamous behavior is nevertheless carried on less formally in brothels, gentlemen's clubs, strip clubs, hotel rooms, the backseat of a car, and any other place that the imagination or memory might lead or recall. Monogamy then can be said to be the exception in society and not the rule.

In my view, humans are dealing with a matter that is bigger than them socially, and a bigger challenge needs a bigger solution. It is my belief that monogamy is not biologically or naturally driven, and it is not controllable by our socialization. Rather, it is my belief that it is spiritually driven, but it is nevertheless, an achievable and realistic expectation for persons in committed relationships. Monogamy is spiritually ordained by the divine to be sustained by the divine. To put it another way, it is God ordained and therefore must be God sustained.

Since the first marriage was between the first man and the first woman, it can logically be assumed that marriage is God's will for everyone with the intention that it would bring the two individuals a deep level of fulfillment and contentment. It was instituted in the beginning, before the fall of man, at a time when man was innocent, and it was designed to be a holy institution. God created monogamy and is therefore the bigger solution; in fact, He is the *only* solution to the monogamy problem. He is the prognosis to the diagnosis we arrived at for the infidelity problem in chapter 2.

A monogamous relationship is the highest and the most noble of human relationships. It underpinned the first institution created by God. It was designed for human beings to function within, because we function best when we are connected to others in a healthy way. In a marriage, the man reflects the strength of God, and the woman reflects the glory of God. When the strength of God marries the glory of God, then the result is a harmonious, productive, and enjoyable state of being where the two become one in purpose, one in faith, and one in love.

When achieved, it is truly gratifying to both parties to the marriage, and greatly admired and honored by God and man. The human benefits of a monogamous relationship are of great value and virtue to the individual stakeholders to the marriage and the society at large. It is a world where there would be no worries of sexually transmitted diseases; it would be a stable and secure place to raise children; it would create a productive and respectable family circle and would normally produce children and a family model after its kind. It is a God idea, and in this idea, He imagined one man for one woman. It is the reason He created only Eve for Adam (not Eve, Eva, and Elaine). Likewise, Eve was given as a helper only to Adam, not to Adam, Allan, and Albert.

When two people in their natural sinful state desire to maintain a successful monogamous life together, each must decide to submit to God's will and His command to love each other selflessly as God has loved us. Hence, although God allowed polygamy in the Old Testament, we can safely conclude that monogamy was still His original intent. The Old Testament does indeed give us scriptural authority in Genesis 1 that marriage between one man and one woman was God's original intention for created man, and that in this original intention He designed our sexual communication to confine itself within a marriage.

Therefore, in conclusion to the discussion in chapter 1, no matter what our personal views may be on polygamy or the issue of what constitutes fornication, Christians, even in their fallen state, ought to strive to the higher calling of the expression of sexual behavior within the confines of a marriage. That being the case, the teachings of the New Testament discouraging polygamy are not so much a contradiction to the Old Testament examples allowing polygamy as they are God restoring us to His original plan (as specified in the Old Testament) to have productive, stable, and strong families and to encourage a socially responsible family life. Hence, regardless of cultural or religious persuasion, it is my belief that when a monogamous relationship is achieved, it is honorable among all people, gives deeper meaning to life, and gives glory to God.

While from a purely natural, biological standpoint, it would almost seem that God expects and understands the tendency for the natural man to lean toward polygamous behavior, He calls forth a physically surrendered, spiritually led man who would dare to put Him first, and He calls that man to a higher order. This call is in the same category as His command to love your enemies, bless those that curse you, and do good to them that despitefully use you. All of these commands are not naturally a function of man; they have a spiritual component. They require a life where flesh is subject to spirit and not the reverse.

It is the person who is completely surrendered and led by the Spirit of God to whom such a behavior as monogamy would come easier and would result in a manifestly changed lifestyle. Just as it is a conscious decision we make to love, it is a conscious decision we make to allow ourselves to be led by the Spirit and not by the flesh. We must learn how to, and then make a conscious decision to deny ourselves of our natural, selfish desires as these become the catalyst for monogamy. Selfishness has no place in love, committed relationships, and marriages.

If we sow to the flesh (or live according to our fleshly desires), then we will reap corruption (i.e., infidelity, dissatisfaction, divorce, unhappiness, and unfulfillment). The flesh is never satisfied, because the more it gets, the more it wants. The want for more is endemic to fleshly living. Further, the complexities of navigating a relationship with many partners is very stressful and does not of itself produce happiness. On the other hand, if we sow to the Spirit (or live according to God's original plan for relationships), then we will reap life everlasting (a good quality of life through a meaningful, sustainable, loving, eternal relationship), which a monogamous relationship was designed to be.

Outside of these critical realizations, a monogamous existence would be unachievable by most. Even born-again believers who do not learn or make the conscious decision to bring their flesh in subjection to their spirit would continue to agonize over monogamy once they refuse to acknowledge that it is not naturally achievable by a boyfriend or girlfriend or a husband or wife; as he or she has a natural disposition to be attracted to members of the opposite sex despite being in an existing committed relationship.

If the natural disposition that lives in the flesh of a person meets with an opportunity, then infidelity is possible. For those reasons, monogamy falls in the category of those marks that most of us must press toward (in the words of the apostle Paul), as it is a high calling of God. It is not achievable merely by one calling himself or herself a Christian (or other religious designation), nor by being saved or by getting married. It is achievable only by living life under the command of the Holy Spirit and not under the commands of the flesh.

For single persons who are not yet married or in a committed relationship, you are not irrelevant in this regard. God's original plan as captured in the book of Genesis provides us with the best reason to be married: a fulfilling, Spirit-led, monogamous relationship in which strong, God-fearing families are raised and produced into society. First Corinthians also indicates to us that it is good for a man not to have sexual relations with a woman, but if sexual immorality would occur, then each man should have sexual relations with his own wife and each woman with her own husband.

As it was God's original design for sexual relations to occur within a marriage between one husband and his wife, engaging in sexual activity outside of this framework usually leads to serious consequences, especially where it occurs with the spouse of another. In Proverbs 6:26–32 (KJV), distinguishing between a prostitute and the wife of another, the Bible states,

For a prostitute can be had for a loaf of bread, but another man's wife preys on your very life. Can a man scoop fire into his lap without his clothes being burned? Can a man walk on hot coals without his feet being scorched? So is he who sleeps with another man's wife; no one who touches her will go unpunished. Men, do not despise a thief if he steal to satisfy his soul when he is hungry; but if he be found, he shall restore sevenfold, he shall give all the substance of his house; But whoso committeth adultery with a woman lacketh understanding: he that doeth it destroyeth his own soul.

There is however, no command or requirement in Scripture that everyone must be married. In fact, the apostle Paul also demonstrated that he favored singleness because it provided a more devoted way to serve God. Singles who do not wish to be married should therefore not feel that they are displeasing God for feeling that way.

There are many single people I know who live happy, long, and fulfilling lives and who find emotional support through avenues other than a spouse (e.g., life net groups, ministry, family, and friends). In 1 Corinthians 7, the apostle Paul was certainly making the point that there are single people who can live a morally pure life in their single state. Singleness, however, should never be used as a state of living in order to encourage and engage in sexual relations outside of God's original intent. If such single persons do not have the high level of self-control required to achieve a pure form of singleness, then it is better to marry than to burn with passion (lust and sexual desire).

There is yet another argument that as long as a person has Jesus in his or her life, then monogamy should be the only way. This brings to my remembrance the Scripture that states that we were all born in sin and shaped in iniquity. Sin and iniquity therefore form part of us from birth. While the choice to sin is made voluntarily by the individual, sinful tendencies are also passed on to us through our DNA without any input from us.

From the Christian perspective, we have all sinned and fallen short of the glory of God, so the infidelity problem is not necessarily one of a person being bad or being destined to be ungodly. The problem is one of sin, and contrary to popular Christian belief, adultery and fornication are not the only sins, nor are they worse than or ranked higher than any other sin. We should therefore be able to discuss truthfully without feeling that the subject matter is off-limits.

It is from the penalty of such sin that born-again believers are being saved. We are progressively being saved from the power of sin and eventually (only after this life is ended), we will be saved from the very presence of sin. Hence, a loving and merciful God does not send someone to hell for eternity because of infidelity or adultery or for any other sin for that matter, regardless of the cause. Hell is reserved for the Devil, his demons, and for sinners who have not accepted that His Son, Jesus Christ, died on the cross for their sins and who do not accept Jesus as their Lord and personal Savior. Sinners who have made this decision to accept Christ are still sinners who will sin, but they are sinners saved by His grace who should continue to feed on the Word and continue pressing toward the mark to perfect his or her salvation.

To those who take exception to these conclusions and believe that monogamy is achievable naturally, this perception may appear justified as it relates to a small minority, but not for the majority. I do agree that there is a small group of humans, both male and female, to whom it comes easy to be with one person at a time—a concept I refer to as serial monogamy—although maybe less so for true monogamy (both of these concepts are discussed in chapter 1). However, when I examine the reason some of these persons have been able to maintain the monogamy model, it perhaps is not as natural as they might think.

If the truth be told, in most cases, it can be traced back to a value system, a moral code, a faith-based or belief system that somewhere along their lifetime and probably from a very early stage, informed their biology and their natural tendencies. For some, their religious beliefs may have been the foundation of this value system and for others, the value system may not have been grounded in religion. Whatever the foundation, when these persons reach adulthood, they then live out what has been instilled in them, as their value system would have superimposed their biological system during the maturity process. It is this value system (and not their biological system) that in the fullness of time became the natural and dominant drive for these persons.

The Bible also provides authority that just as sin can be passed on from generation to generation, so can good morals and ethics. The apostle Paul in speaking to Timothy about his faithfulness in 2 Timothy 1:5 (NIV) said to him, "I am reminded of your sincere faith, which first lived in your grandmother Lois and in your mother Eunice and, I am persuaded, now lives in you also." As a result of various factors influencing biology, although absolute monogamy is not innate due to the fallen state of man, it becomes easier for these persons in whom this value system, moral code, faith/belief system has become the dominant drive, to practice monogamy more consistently.

To conclude this chapter, I propose that living a monogamous life successfully hinges significantly on a life lived in the Spirit. If we are serious in achieving it, this requires living a life that places a person's affection toward God and not toward his or her own desires. In this Spirit-led life approach, it would be believed, as King Solomon proposed in the book of Ecclesiastes, that nothing, no matter what it is—money, power, a multitude of women, riches, and the like—fulfills except God. It is all meaningless but for God.

Hence, in this Spirit-led life, if God commands me to be a one-woman man for life, then I would accept that any deviation from that plan would corrupt God's intent. Further, because of my understanding that my ultimate fulfillment must come from God and because of my love for Him, I obey Him and I want to please Him. Since I understand that His original intent was for me to have one woman, my being monogamous is no longer about my natural inclinations or what is common to mankind; it becomes purely about God and pleasing Him. Consequently, my male sex drive does not continuously become a hindrance to my faithfulness in my marriage, and my faithfulness to my wife comes from an outflow of my love for God, so I work continuously to control my flesh by elevating my spirit life. My wife then becomes a direct beneficiary of my relationship with, and my love for my heavenly Father.

Love in this manner is love at its best, love par excellence; it is love that accurately reflects 1 Corinthians 13. It is love we should all strive to achieve. It can truly be described as *a beautiful love*.

CHAPTER 10
A Word to the Young

From My Heart

Life has taught me many lessons; some of those lessons have been very costly but also proved to be of great value. It is from these lessons learned over my fifty-plus years of life that I have shared in this book, and in conclusion I offer some final guidance to the young. I accept my responsibility as a bishop, pastor, former youth pastor, counselor, father, and friend to do my part in ensuring that future generations of young people are as best equipped as possible in their pursuit of meaningful, interpersonal relationships.

It is important to have successful relationships, but unfortunately for us, these relationships are not acquired (with cash or kind), inherited (from our parents or guardians), or conveyed (by our pastors or the wedding ceremony); nor do they happen magically or wishfully. They must be built with strong material in order to withstand the vicissitudes of life, and as with anything that requires building, such relationships require a strong foundation. Fundamentally, they cannot be built without the labor and love of the two parties to the relationship.

Against the backdrop of all the forgoing chapters, I now offer young people some specific guidance that can assist them in avoiding the pitfalls that so many of us who have gone before have fallen into and which derailed us on our journey in pursuit of the monogamous model that God intended in the beginning.

I have not come to these conclusions, nor am I qualified to offer them because I got it right in my own interpersonal relationships. In fact, the reason I can offer the guidance I am offering is because I got it wrong in my relationship life, and in getting it wrong, I am now able to understand and analyze what should have been done by me and my marriage partner and what could be done for others who want to make the best attempt at "getting it right."

I share with you also that I spent many years agonizing over my relationship life. There have been times when I felt like a failure as a pastor as a result of my failed marriages, and I genuinely regret the consequences the failure of my first marriage caused my children. I have struggled with feeling worthy enough to lead people, since I was never able to set the perfect example or be the perfect example for them. I was bound by the realities of experiencing failure in this one aspect of my life … this one thing, has been real for me.

Yet I am aware of the many biblical Scriptures that encourage us when we make mistakes. James 3:2 clearly acknowledges that we all stumble in many ways and that anyone who is never at fault in what he or she says is perfect and is able to keep his or her whole body in check. I do not claim to be perfect, and I have accepted my faults.

Therefore, like the apostle Paul stated in Philippians 3:12 (NIV), "It is not that I have already obtained all this or have already arrived at my goal, but I still press on to take hold of that for which Christ Jesus took hold of me." I have also found comfort in the promise in Psalm 37:24 that though I stumble, I will not fall, for I know that the Lord upholds my hand. I am also comfortable in sharing my heart with you in this very important chapter of this book as I have a promise in Proverbs 28:13 that whoever conceals his transgressions will not prosper, but he who confesses and forsakes them will obtain mercy; and also in Proverbs 24:16 that says that the righteous falls seven times and rises again but the wicked stumbles in times of calamity.

Hence, as I look back over my life in preparation to offer this guidance to future generations, I adopt the words of the apostle Paul in Philippians 3:13–14: I do not consider that I have made it through the challenges on my own. But one thing I do: forgetting what lies behind and straining forward to what lies ahead. I continue to press toward the mark for the prize of the high calling of God in Jesus Christ.

Sex Is Not Love
I might as well start at what has now become the forefront of relationship focus for young people: the issue of sex and confusing passionate sex for love. For the young women especially, I urge you to understand that most young men at a young age do not know what true love and commitment is all about. Their desire for relationship is purely driven by a natural sexual appetite, which can be fulfilled by one, two, three, or four women at any one time.

In fulfilling this desire for young men, young women make themselves as special as the moment of the sexual encounter and nothing more. I know that this is hard for them to hear, but it is the truth. Simply put, men do not ascribe the same value to sex as women do. As I discussed in earlier chapters, the desire for sex by men is driven from a basic, natural, biological need, while for most women, it completes the fulfillment of a wider emotional need.

The result of this mismatch in value placing often brings about much disillusion and hurt, which to a young and impressionable heart and spirit can cause severe emotional consequences when navigating their way around interpersonal relationships. Young women therefore ought to be aware of this and acknowledge when they are being sought out by young men whose main objective in the relationship is not to get to know them, care for them, and/or be concerned about their best interests, but to encourage or demand sexual intimacy as a requirement for the subsistence of the relationship.

Look for Love in All the Right Places

In the Song of Solomon, King Solomon urged the daughters of Jerusalem not to awaken love (eros) before its time. Once romance or sexual intimacy is awakened, then it is hard to sedate it. By the time most young people are ready to settle down in a committed long-term relationship for life, they have a long list of "ex's" (ex-boyfriends, ex-girlfriends, ex-whatever the designation)—persons they have already been intimate with, many of whom they wished they had never met.

Sex is one of the greatest needs of mankind and is also one of the strongest desires of our being. However, as King Solomon suggests, premature romance can lead to a lifetime of hurt, regret, and unfulfillment. God did not design our relationship lives to be this way, and it was to protect us from these negative consequences that He designed those lives to operate within certain parameters. In order to assist a person with being faithful in his or her marriage, the starting point should be fidelity in his or her dating life. In order to do so successfully, he or she must have a strong personal and committed relationship with God and believe in His original plan for monogamous relationships.

Young people should also be mindful of the information they rely upon to inform their relationship decision-making. For example, Internet-based pornography, secular movies and television programs, secular love magazines and the like, are not appropriate learning tools on God's idea of love. The best learning tools for love, God's way, are the Holy Bible or other biblically based resources.

If young people expose themselves to pornography, illicit sex programs and stories that suggest open relationships, free love (without commitment) and same-sex relationships, then their lives will pattern these teachings, because their behavior will be impacted by the information received in these media. Biblical models of a godly relationship can instead be found in Ephesians 5 and Proverbs 31:10–31 (for ease of reference, these two passages are discussed in detail in chapter 6). While Ephesians 5 offers a more theoretical model, Proverbs 31 offers a practical model of how the relationship should function and the results of implementing and adhering to such a model. Importantly also, the foundation of any lasting, viable relationship is predicated on friendship.

As I discussed in chapter 8, friendship stands upon four main pillars. They are *acceptance* (as you are), *respect* (in spite of who you are), *trust* (who you are), and *love* (because of who you are). Any lasting and enjoyable relationship can be built on such a strong and resisting foundation. Let me re-emphasize then, that it cannot be built only on romance, eroticism, or passion (romantic love).

I know of many persons who had relationships that started out with romance and passion off the charts—romance that took them to the moon and back, so much so that they never thought anything else could possibly be required to sustain the relationship. Many of those persons consummated marriage relationships on this premise and are still not together today. In my younger years, I too shared that view; but I have now lived long enough to share with you that romantic love, as beautiful and magical as it may seem at the time, is too fragile and too temporal a foundation to build a lasting, meaningful relationship upon.

The Importance of Absolute Acceptance
It is vitally important for us to accept that we are all a sum total of our experiences, and each person in a relationship must accept the other person for who they have become by the time they form a relationship with them. Don't be under any illusion that you can change a person by what you give them, do for them, or promise them. Young men,

please be aware in particular, that material things do not buy love nor do they satisfy the emotional needs of women. All the excitement material needs bring will ever only satisfy a temporary desire. Young women, likewise, the provision of sex in abundance (even great sex), good cooking, excellent household management, flawless upkeep of your physical appearance and perfectly raising a man's children on their own do not guarantee faithfulness in a man who has a disposition to be unfaithful.

The Bible does declare in Jeremiah 13:23 (NIV), "Can an Ethiopian change his skin or a leopard, his spots?" People are who they are, and if you would like to know the true character of people, then learn their history, hurts, hopes, and hearts. Do not be fooled by the fine, beautiful or handsome outward appearances you meet at the initial stage, because that person is not the one with whom the relationship will be lived. On the contrary, open, genuine, and honest conversation with a person can create a comfortable atmosphere and will eventually reveal the true character of that person. As the late Maya Angelou said, "If a person shows you who they are, believe them." Do not think that you can change who they are or ignore who they show you they are—believe them.

Once you have believed them, the next step is to determine if you can accept what you have now believed about them. If the answer is yes, then you may proceed. If the answer is no, then do not proceed or proceed with major caution. Know for sure also, that this "knowing period" is not an overnight thing. Take time to know him or her, as very rarely will the real person ever be comfortable enough to show up at the beginning of the discovery stages of the relationship.

I stress the importance of acceptance as a prerequisite in taking the relationship to another level, because I have seen many young people embarking on life with knowledge of the obvious flaws of their partners, intent on changing their partners' behavior. The intention is usually a recipe for disaster because persons do not change easily simply upon the insistence of someone else. In fact, in most cases, the person that change is being enforced upon may become upset and frustrated with and withdrawn from the person trying to effect the change, feeling that they are not good enough for the partner who is trying to change him or her. It is important to understand very early in your young lives that only God can bring about real and lasting change in a person, and He can only do so with the willingness of the person in respect of which the change is required.

The Respect Requirement
Respect is also a mandatory requirement in building life-lasting relationships. In my teachings, I demonstrate three basic ways to determine whether there is respect between the parties in a relationship: (1) the way they talk to each other, (2) the way they touch each other, and (3) the way they treat each other. As an illustration, if a man is cursing his wife or girlfriend, using profanity in his arguments with her, calling her names and referring to her by derogatory terms, then this is a sure sign that he does not respect her, and it is an absolute red alert in the relationship.

By the same token, a woman would normally disrespect a man by belittling him, whether it is by her actions (body language) or her words, answering back in unkind, harsh, and hurtful words or willfully acting in a manner that she knows the man finds disrespectful. Men who experience this type of behavior from women should take notice of it. In my own experience, it only amplifies as the relationship progresses.

One partner in a relationship will also know if the other partner respects him or her by the way the one partner handles/touches the other. If the physical touch or handling is abusive, then there is clearly no respect by the partner who is touching abusively for the partner to whom the abusive touch is directed. How a person is treated is also an important determinant in detecting respect.

In his book, *The 5 Love Languages*, Gary Chapman explains that the secret to love that lasts is contained in five main love languages. They are words of affirmation, quality time, receiving gifts, acts of service, and physical touch. While relationships work best if each party discovers the partner's primary love language so that he or she can communicate with the partner using that partner's preferred love language, one partner in a relationship can use any of these five determinants to ascertain whether the partner's treatment of him or her is respectful.

Respect is a mandatory requirement in relationship building. As Dr. Emerson Eggerichs suggests in his book *Love & Respect*, a woman who does not feel loved will generally withhold her respect, and a man who does not feel respected will usually withhold his love. This conundrum creates a vicious cycle of lack in the relationship with blame continuously going back and forth in either direction. The resulting chaos, frustration, and deterioration will (unless treated in time) eat away like a cancer, at every other aspect of the relationship—trust, friendship, acceptance, and eventually love—until no aspect of the foundation is left upon which the relationship can be sustained or rebuilt.

The Truth of Trust

Trust in a relationship is the most fragile of the tenets of friendship. It is usually the first to enter the door (other things being equal) when two people meet and usually the first to exit also. Many of us remember the rhyme, "Humpty Dumpty." Trust is like Humpty Dumpty when he had the great fall. When trust is broken, all the king's horses and all the king's men cannot put it back together again.

I am not absolutely convinced however, that Humpty Dumpty could not be put back together. In the rhyme, it is important to note that no one bothered to call the king to see if Humpty Dumpty could be fixed by him. It might have been the king and only the king who could put Humpty Dumpty together again. So too in our relationship lives, when trust is broken, I believe and I have seen that it could be fully restored. But in my experience, God (the King) and godly counsel are extremely vital in restoring such a broken trust.

Love

In chapter 6, the love requirement and the types of love are addressed at length. The need to not fall in love but instead understand it, as discussed in that chapter is very relevant to young people as well, and I urge you to read it carefully and understand it. The love God designed for us in our relationships speaks to the type of love spoken about in 1 Corinthians 13:4–7 (NIV):

> Love is patient, love is kind. It does not envy, it does not boast, it is not proud. It does not dishonor others, it is not self-seeking, it is not easily angered, it keeps no record of wrongs. Love does not delight in evil but rejoices with the truth. It always protects, always trusts, always hopes, always perseveres.

This love is not romantic love. It is not fleeting nor does it require passion to operate effectively and with sustainability. It is the type of love that says, I like you; I want to spend time with you; I like being where you are; I like talking to you; I like sharing my time with you, I like helping you; I like when you help me; I just like you. In this type of pure love, romance would not be the impetus of a person's love for another. The liking for the person, while it may be inclusive of romance, is reflective of a deeper and more sustainable love. It is on this type of love that fruitful, long-lasting, comfortable, easy, and fulfilling relationships will and can be built.

Honesty Is the Best Policy

Honesty is also a necessary requirement for young people embarking on love relationships for life. They must therefore force honest discussions about life in the areas where life is really lived. They should discuss and settle on major issues likely to form a part of their life plans, including their views on faith (inclusive of religion), family (children, children's education, and the role of in-laws), finances (financial planning, savings, investment, setting financial goals), and friends (setting boundaries).

I have counseled too many people and have seen too many of my friends end up divorced when after years in a marriage, they realize that their opposing views on these major issues cannot be easily settled, and these unsettled issues eventually drive a wedge in the unity of the relationship. These issues are obviously too important to ignore.

Importantly, a person's views on faith will determine how the household will be managed and how the children will be raised from a religious perspective. It will also affect the issue of tithing, and many couples have significant marriage problems where one spouse tithes 10 percent of the family income, while the other spouse is not in agreement with this.

Whether or not children will be introduced to the relationship should also be settled, as many husbands find themselves married to wives who had no intentions of having children, much to the distress of their husbands (who did not learn this until after they were married, since (taken for granted by one party or the other) no discussion or settlement to any such discussion was had)! Likewise, how the children will be educated (whether publicly or privately) should be settled because this would impact the finances and the financial planning of the household in a significant way.

There should be discussions on how the finances of the family will be planned and organized, contributions to savings, and how investments will be approached in general. It is also important to set boundaries for the involvement of both in-laws and friends in the marriage. Both are crucial categories of people in our lives, but they have equally contributed quite significantly to the breakdown of many marriages.

The new and young couple should therefore discuss, agree and actively manage the limit of their involvement in the marriage.

God Is Critical in the Mix
In addition to all the above guidance, it goes without saying that God must remain the constant. Consider these three proverbs:

1. A family that prays together, stays together.
As I have indicated in the previous chapter, monogamy is a God idea, and if it is God ordained then it needs to be God sustained. One of the main tools given to sustain spiritual living is prayer. When we pray for each other, we serve each other, we build each other up, and we encourage each other. In prayer, one touches three worlds: God in worship (maintaining our relationship with God); Satan in warfare (defending against the enemy of godly things); and man in works (two people praying for each other for the well-being of the relationship).

The practice of prayer then becomes effective and enables spiritual tolerance, as it is hard to tear down someone you are praying to build up. In other words, it is hard for a husband and wife to dislike each other if they are constantly in prayer for and with each other.

2. No God, no peace. Know God, know peace.
Where there is no God, then it will be hard to find peace in your life, but when you know God, then you will know peace. It is therefore important to pursue and develop a personal relationship with God. Accept Jesus as your Lord and personal Savior, let Him live and abide in your heart, and allow Him to control your spirit. Also allowing God to take a headship position in your marriage or relationship will create a peaceful atmosphere for the relationship.

3. If you forget God, then Satan will rule.
It is when Adam and Eve decided to go against God (ignore God's instructions) that Satan was allowed to enter into their relationship.

The same is true today. If we ignore God, it leaves the door open for Satan to wreak havoc in our lives in general. Our relationship/married lives are no exception to this rule. Ecclesiastes 12:1 urges the young to remember the Creator in the days of their youth. Do this and live abundant lives.

CHAPTER 11
Mystery Solved!

My conclusion regarding the mystery that surrounds monogamy is therefore very simple, and it is a conclusion that makes the most sense to me, given the preponderance of evidence presented in this book and from many other sources:

> Monogamy is not natural, nor is it common among men. It is spiritual and ordained by God to be sustained by God. Those who seek to have their relationship lives directed and guided by godly principles will find a monogamous existence a haven of rest.

EPILOGUE

There is absolutely nothing in life that challenges us more than our interpersonal relationships. Furthermore, there is nothing that challenges interpersonal relationships more than infidelity. In this book, we have raised the discussion about monogamy and the human challenge of being monogamous. We have asked many thought-provoking questions, chief of which is whether it is natural to be monogamous or whether we are in direct conflict with our very nature as we aim to be. We have also discussed how societal constructs do not support the noble idea of being monogamous.

We concluded that if monogamy is anything, it is spiritual—of a higher standard of living, not common among man. The onus is now on the readers to have an honest and open discussion with your friends, your loved ones, and your significant other/spouse about this much-avoided subject. I urge you to lay down your guard, take off the gloves, and talk about it. You will find that the truth will set you free—or at least make you light.

There is one thing we know for sure: infidelity is not going away. You cannot wish it away, marry it away, cry it away, or even fight it away. It is even hard to truly pray it away if your prayers are not followed by a strong commitment to the God-idea of monogamy.

At this point, I would like to reiterate my caution to those who may read this book and seek to use it as a license to be promiscuous and unfaithful in their relationships. Please understand that this is not the intent. It was simply intended to raise the discussion at a serious level and to force each of us, including the church, to retreat from our current, unhelpful stance and analyze the situation from an unprejudiced perspective. I do acknowledge and can identify with the challenge that being monogamous presents to the best of us, both male and female. Can it be attained? I believe it is attainable. As I mentioned in an earlier chapter, it has been practiced and is being practiced by many, and when it is achieved, it can truly be a *beautiful love*.

I now leave you to ponder the words of the poetic, wise man, King Solomon as he illustrates a beautiful love between two lovers in Song of Solomon 2, 4 and 7 (NIV):

Beloved (She)
I am a rose of Sharon, a lily of the valleys.

Lover (He)
Like a lily among thorns is my darling among the maidens.

Beloved
Like an apple tree among the trees of the forest is my lover among the young men.
I delight to sit in his shade and his fruit is sweet to my taste.
He has taken me to the banquet hall, and his banner over me is love.
Strengthen me with raisins, refresh me with apples, for I am faint with love.
His left arm is under my head and his right arm embraces me.
Daughters of Jerusalem, I charge you by the gazelles and by the does of the field: Do not arouse or awaken love unless it so desires.
Lover
My dove in the clefts of the rock, in the hiding places on the mountainside, show me your face, let me hear your voice; for your voice is sweet, and your face is lovely.

Beloved
My lover is mine and I am his; he browses among the lilies.

Lover
How beautiful you are, my darling!
Oh, how beautiful!
Your eyes behind your veil are doves.
Your hair is like royal tapestry; the king is held captive by its tresses.
Your teeth are like a flock of sheep just shorn, coming up from the washing.
Each has its own twin, not one of them is alone.
Your lips are like scarlet ribbon; your mouth is lovely.
Your temples behind your veil are like the halves of a pomegranate.
Your neck is like an ivory tower, the tower of David, built with elegance, on it hang a thousand shields, all of them shields of warriors.
How beautiful your sandaled feet, O princes daughter!
Your graceful legs are like jewels, the work of a craftsman's hands.
Your navel is a rounded goblet that never lacks blended wine.
Your waist is a mount of wheat encircled by lilies.
Your eyes are the pool of Heshbon by the gate of Bath Rabbim.
Your nose is like the tower of Lebanon looking towards Damascus.
Your two breasts are like two fawns, the twin fawns of a gazelle that browse among the lilies …
All beautiful you are, my darling; there is no flaw in you.

Your head crowns you like Mount Carmel.
You have stolen my heart, my sister my bride; you have stolen my heart with one glance of your eyes, with one jewel of your necklace.
How delightful is your love, my sister, my bride!
How much more pleasing is your love than wine and the fragrance of your perfume than any spice!
Your lips drop sweetness as the honeycomb my bride; milk and honey are under your tongue.
The fragrance of your garments is like that of Lebanon.

You are a garden locked up, my sister, my bride, you are a spring enclosed, a sealed fountain.
Your plants are an orchard of pomegranates with choice fruits, with henna and nard, and saffron, calamus and cinnamon, with every kind of incense tree, with myrrh and aloes and all the finest spices.
You are a garden fountain, a well of flowing water streaming down from Lebanon.
How beautiful you are and how pleasing, O love, with your delights!
Your stature is like that of a palm, and your breasts like clusters of fruit.
I said, "I will climb the palm tree;
I will take hold of its fruit."

Beloved
Awake, north wind, south wind!
Blow on my garden, that its fragrance may spread abroad.
Let my lover come into his garden and taste its choice fruits.

APPENDIX

Survey on Monogamy/Infidelity

1. How important is it for you to be faithful (monogamous) in a relationship?
   ☐ Extremely important
   ☐ Somewhat important
   ☐ Neutral
   ☐ Somewhat unimportant
   ☐ Extremely unimportant

2. Do you think too much importance is put on the need for fidelity (or being faithful) in relationships?
   ☐ Yes, what's the big deal? Who cares anyway?
   ☐ Yes, people should care about faithfulness, but they go overboard.
   ☐ It seems people generally are well-balanced about their views regarding fidelity.
   ☐ No, people should put more emphasis on fidelity.
   ☐ No, people seem to pay fidelity no mind; they should put a much greater emphasis on the need for fidelity in a relationship.

3. Is it natural for a man to feel that he should have the opportunity to sleep with more than one woman at any one point in time?
   ☐ Yes
   ☐ No

4. Is it natural for a woman to feel that she should have the opportunity to sleep with more than one man at any one point in time?
   ☐ Yes
   ☐ No

5. Do you think the need for fidelity/faithfulness should only be relevant to married couples?
   ☐ Yes **(skip the next two questions)**
   ☐ No

   If yes, why?
   _____
   _____
   _____

6. Do you also think committed couples (boyfriend/girlfriend type relationships) should be faithful to each other?
   ☐ Yes
   ☐ No

   (a) If yes, why?
   _____
   _____
   _____

   (b) If no, why not?
   _____
   _____
   _____

7. If you answered no to the previous question, what type of couples should be faithful to each other?

_____
_____
_____

8. Have you ever been unfaithful in a marriage or committed relationship?
   ☐ Yes
   ☐ No

   If yes, what would you say was the reason?

   _____
   _____
   _____

9. Have you ever or would you ever have an affair?
   ☐ Yes, I have had an affair.
   ☐ I would NEVER have an affair.
   ☐ I have never had an affair, but it's possible I may have one in the future.

   Why would you never have an affair, or if you would, what would cause you to have an affair?

   _____
   _____
   _____
   _____
   _____

   *Please answer question 10 only if you have NEVER had an affair.

10. Do you think you would possibly have an affair if you were 100 percent certain that you would not get caught?
☐ Yes
☐ No

Please answer question 11 only if you HAVE had an affair or been unfaithful in a relationship.

11. Have you ever been unfaithful while in a committed relationship?
_____
_____
_____

Did you feel guilt while having the affair or after the affair?
☐ Yes
☐ No

What would you say caused or led to the affair?
_____
_____
_____

12. Do you think most people would have affairs if they knew they would not be caught?
☐ Yes
☐ No

13. Have you been physically or emotionally attracted to anyone other than your spouse or committed partner?
☐ Yes
☐ No

If yes, how did you handle it?
_____
_____
_____

14. Is there anything your partner could do to ensure that you remain faithful?
_____
_____
_____

15. What do you think is the aim of encouraging fidelity in relationships?
_____
_____
_____

16. Would you carry on a relationship with a woman/man who has been unfaithful to you?
☐ Yes
☐ No

17. Would you seek revenge by returning the favor if your partner is unfaithful to you?
☐ Yes
☐ No

18. Has your partner/spouse ever cheated or been unfaithful to you?
☐ Yes
☐ No **(skip the next two questions)**

19. How does it make you feel that your partner or spouse cheated on you?
_____
_____
_____

20. How did having your partner or spouse cheat on you affect the relationship?
_____
_____
_____

21. Do you think people can have more meaningful relationships if they were open relationships (each person does as either pleases with his or her sex life but both manage the household and the children)?
    ☐ Yes
    ☐ No

22. Do you think marriages should have a renewal date, say every five years (so as to give an option to leave) instead of divorce?
    ☐ Yes
    ☐ No

23. Would you prefer to live in society where it is legal for you to have more than one spouse?
    ☐ Yes
    ☐ No

24. Would you be comfortable if your wife or husband had another spouse beside you?
    ☐ Yes
    ☐ No

25. If you have ever had fear of infidelity occurring in your relationship, how has it affected your relationship?
_____
_____

26. What is your gender?
    ☐ Male
    ☐ Female

27. Are you currently married?
    ☐ Yes
    ☐ No

28. If you are not married, are you in a committed relationship?
    ☐ Yes
    ☐ No

29. How old are you?
    ☐ 20 or under
    ☐ 21–40
    ☐ 41–55
    ☐ 56–70
    ☐ 71 or over

AFTERWORD

I grew up in a time when the church's voice was silent as it relates to the many parameters of what were to be inclusive to a healthy and productive relationship. The mere mentioning of sex was strongly forbidden, never taught about. There was no room or place for dating; and in the midst of conventions, conferences, Sunday school, youth meetings, and other church-related gatherings, if questions were ever offered to be answered in relationship as to: *How do you know it's the right boy or the right girl?; What do I do with these feelings?*, the immediate response was, "You young people are just fast, mannish, or just hot between the legs." What came out of those times was a conclusion that sex was nasty. It was a dirty thing. So we referred to having sex as doing the nasty, when in fact, it was quite the opposite; and the church's response, even today, has not changed.

The irony is that while our desire for intimacy and closeness is funneled through our biology and so handled by us in our natural state, intimacy and sexual desire is an ultimate creation by God Himself. There are therefore some much deeper insights that must be discussed on the issue of monogamy, and I believe that the writer is at his best summoning the call for a much more intelligent and productive conversation. I am lending my voice and pen to the same, hoping to encourage a more open discussion between men and women of all ethnicities.

There was a study done on lovebirds, and it is said that they practice social monogamy (i.e., the raising of a family with one mate while enjoying romantic rendezvous every now and then). Some scientists have concluded that such behavior is helpful, ensuring survival of the species. There was another study that indicates that less than half of all modern societies forbid extramarital relationships. In fact many cultures don't see affairs as deal breakers to a successful marriage. Now, while this may make interesting conversation, I'm going to say that I'm not buying it as the conclusion of any such discussion, as it does not add up to God's original purpose and plan for His creation. I agree that after the fall of man, fidelity was molested and almost hijacked out of our society. There was a loss of innocence; but not because someone is mannish, hot, wild, or wants to sow their oats. I would suggest that it is because of an eternal struggle between the flesh and the spirit.

The truth is, as the author highlights, marriage isn't just about sex; it is about things much deeper and more lasting than sex. Furthermore, it is also my belief that it is an unjust expectation for persons to rely upon their marriage partner to fulfill every aspect of who they are, as marriage is not designed to do this. Such an expectation is simply the prescription to have your heart broken and shattered. Such voids can only be filled by God, and one should therefore come to the marriage fulfilled—a whole person, intellectually, socially, and spiritually. In order to have successful relationships, couples must continue to grow as individuals and together. If not, their true intimate relationship will be short-lived.

No matter what may have been the symptom of a divorce, the real cause is usually the lack of consideration and the insensitivity to or misunderstanding of one or one another's needs and purpose. Now, there are some dogs out there, but for the most part I'm referring to those who want to do it right. It is my heartfelt desire that we, with intentionality, insert this type of dialogue into our community, into our churches, and into our teachings. Let this be the beginning of many open discussions using voice tone that allows us to hear with our hearts and not just our ears.

I pray that this book becomes the talking point in dating, premarital and post-marital discussions, and even a guide as persons walk out this journey called relationship. May the readers have new discoveries and even greater inspiration. Remember, what's been given to us is a gift, and this gift can be successfully realized if we go back to the manufacturer's instructions; how *He* intended for each of us to get the best and the most out of *His* creative design.

Finally, one of the greatest needs in society is the need for mentorship. Little boys and girls are going to emulate someone, something. So it is important that we continually place before them real-life models, exampling what it means to stand, not only in times of joyful celebration but in times of stress, challenge, and adversity. There is even now a little boy and a little girl in all of us looking to be influenced. I pray that *The Monogamy Mystery* influences each reader on these very important issues that plague many of us in our interpersonal relationships.

—Bishop Joseph A. McCargo

ABOUT THE AUTHOR

Bishop John I. Cline is the senior pastor of the New Life Baptist Church in Tortola, British Virgin Islands. At the age of seventeen, he left the shores of the British Virgin Islands to pursue tertiary education and greater exposure and opportunities in the United States of America by way of the United States Virgin Islands. He pursued his tertiary training in Framingham, Massachusetts, in electronic engineering. Upon completion of his training, he then relocated to Bloomfield, New Jersey, where he was licensed to preach and began his ministry in 1985 at the New Light Baptist Church where Reverend C. Hall (of blessed memory) presided as senior pastor. While at New Light, he served in the capacities as associate minister and youth pastor. In this capacity, one of his chief accomplishments was launching the church's first ministry to the homeless.

In 1989, following his ordination as a pastor, he was led to return to the British Virgin Islands and continued his ministry in the capacity as youth pastor at the Cane Garden Bay Baptist Church in Tortola. In 1993, he was called to act in the capacity as senior pastor to the Road Town Baptist Church, a call he willingly accepted. The church grew under his leadership by leaps and bounds and in 1995, it acquired property upon which to construct new premises for the church. In February of 1997, the church broke ground and nine months later the building was dedicated and the church was renamed The New Life Baptist Church. He continues today to serve New Life as its senior pastor.

Bishop Cline is a leader with a vision and firmly believes that as children of the living God, we must impact the world, not just spiritually but socially and physically as well. Passionate about this vision, in the year 2000, the idea of a New Life Day Care was downloaded to him. The main focus was to ensure that children in the British Virgin Islands community were receiving early tuition in biblical teachings as well as in their academic journey. A second building was therefore constructed and dedicated to house the New Life Day Care Centre. The day care opened its doors in September 2000 and subsequently expanded to include a preschool a year later in 2001. The now New Life Day Care & Learning Centre is geared toward children from three months to seven years old. It adopts the British education system and thereby provides tuition and instruction for preprimary-aged students up to Stage II. The population of the day care and learning center to date approximates 105 students.

In 2003, NLBC spread its mission to Africa where it supports a church in Nairobi, Kenya. NLBC has also pledged its financial support to a school administered by the church in Kenya and in appreciation of this generosity, the school was named the Tortola Child Rescue and Learning Centre. Together, the partnership has seen the growth of the primary school from 20 students to nearly three hundred students at present. Bishop Cline, (together with members of NLBC and members of the BVI professional community including contractors, architects, and the like), traveled to Kenya in July 2014 and began the construction of the secondary school which will enable the primary school students to continue their education at the secondary level.

In October 2005, he was consecrated to the Office of the Bishop, and inducted into the College of Bishops as a presbyter, adjudicator, and an examiner. With his mind-set to impact the British Virgin Islands community, in 2011, Bishop Cline acted upon a vision as he embarked on the construction of a recreational facility that would mainly target the youth generation—a generation that he feels is in dire need of attention and rescue. In November 2012, the recreational facility was constructed and dedicated and is now in daily operation. The multimillion-dollar facility is approximately thirty thousand square feet and houses a gymnasium with modern, state-of-the-art workout equipment, a full-size basketball/volleyball court, a children's playroom and café, a six-lane bowling alley, conference facilities, a ballroom, and a learning center. As the visionary for the Save the Seed Energy Centre, Bishop Cline believes that the multipurpose sport facility will help to create an impact in the British Virgin Islands community by providing a safe and productive environment for young people to congregate and engage in wholesome and enriching activities.

In furthering its commitment to the Great Commission, the church also has a televangelism arm, and televises its services not only on the island of Tortola, but also in other islands in the Caribbean including St. Kitts, St. Vincent, Anguilla, and Jamaica. Its annual Healing and Deliverance Crusade and its annual Power Plus Crusade are also streamed internationally and have developed quite a large following of persons, including the New Life diaspora, all of whom are very appreciative of the efforts New Life makes to ensure that even those persons who could not be physically present could be spiritually fed.

He is also the founding member of the New Life Baptist Church Foundation. The foundation was legally established in October 2011 to facilitate charitable endeavors. Other missionary endeavors of the New Life Baptist Church as spearheaded by Bishop Cline include the commissioning and construction of the facilities which house the Emanuel Baptist Church in Virgin Gorda as well as the provision of financial support to the Boys Home in St. Kitts, West Indies.

An avid and dedicated businessman, Bishop Cline is also the cofounder and president of Infinite Solutions, a BVI business company, through which he successfully trades consumer electronics and associated services in the British Virgin Islands. He is also the founder, president, and managing director of Atlantis Solar, a BVI business company through which he successfully markets, promotes, and distributes alternative energy products locally, regionally, and internationally.

Known for his love for God, his compassion for people, his undeniable business prowess and acumen, Bishop Cline was appointed to the British Virgin Islands Health Services Authority (the Authority) in March 2012 where he presently serves as chairman of the board of directors of the Authority. Bishop Cline attributes his success to the influence of godly parents, strong family ties, a caring church, and a supportive community. He desires to "pass it on!"

Is there a book inside of you? Ever wanted to self publish but didn't know how? Concerned about the financial part of self publishing? Relax. Take a deep breath. We can help!

Finally! An affordable Self Publishing company for all of your Self Publishing needs. We have the right services, with the right prices with the right quality. So, what are you waiting for?

Unpack those dreams, break out that pen, your dreams of getting published may not be so far off after all!

Jasher Press & Co. is here to provide you with Consulting, Book Formatting, Cover Designs, Editing services but most importantly inspiration to bring your dreams to past.

And this whole process can be done in less than 90 days! You thought about it, you talked about it but now is the time!

www.jasherpress.com
1-888-220-2068
customerservice@jasherpress.com